cirencester
college
a beacon college

The
Connell Guide
to
Shakespeare's
Second Tetralogy

Richard II
Henry IV Parts 1 and 2
Henry V

cirencest
college
a beacon college

Contents

NOTES

HOUSE OF PLANTAGENET FAMILY TREE

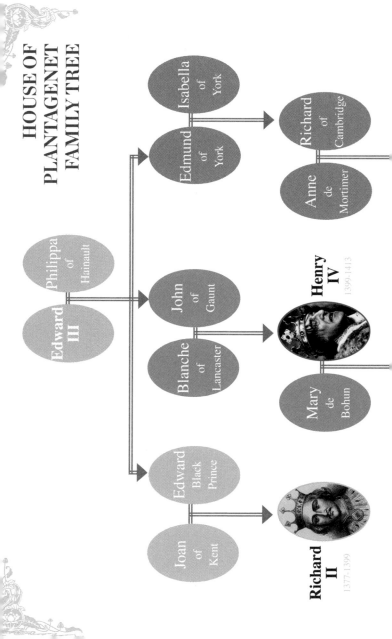

Edward III — Philippa of Hainault

Edward Black Prince — Joan of Kent

John of Gaunt — Blanche of Lancaster

Edmund of York — Isabella of York

Richard of Cambridge — Anne de Mortimer

Richard II 1377-1399

Henry IV 1399-1413 — Mary de Bohun

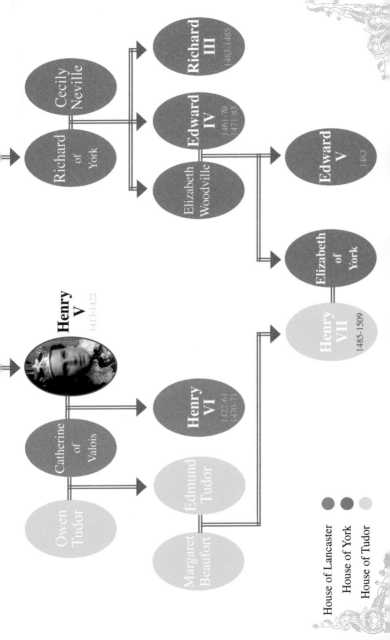

Henry V
1413-1422

Richard of York

Cecily Neville

Richard III
1483-1485

Edward IV
1461-70
1471-83

Elizabeth Woodville

Edward V
1483

Catherine of Valois

Owen Tudor

Henry VI
1422-61
1470-71

Edmund Tudor

Margaret Beaufort

Elizabeth of York

Henry VII
1485-1509

● House of Lancaster
● House of York
● House of Tudor

Introduction

In his first tetralogy of history plays (*Henry VI Parts 1, 2 and 3*, and *Richard III*), Shakespeare offered the most extensive dramatic sequence since the great days of ancient Greek drama in Athens.

In the early years of his career, around 1589-93, it is evident that the young Shakespeare had nerve, verve and cheek. The sheer range of his early works implies a pugnacious generic virtuosity: he seemed to be challenging predecessors and rivals in a wide variety of genres. These included: verse-narratives on classical subjects; the amatory sonnet-sequence; farcical comedy; and gory revenge-drama.

Shakespeare then wrote not one play but three on the doomed reign of Henry VI, capping it with *Richard III*, in which Richard is vigorously demonised. Evidently the theatre-goers of the day demanded more of the same. (History plays were very popular. Marlowe's *Tamburlaine the Great* was so successful that it generated a sequel, portraying Tamburlaine's death.)

No wonder that by 1592 Shakespeare was being denounced by a rival, Robert Greene, as "an upstart Crow, beautified with our feathers", who is "an absolute *Iohannes Factotum* [Jack of all trades]". The significance of the sheer scale of that first historical tetralogy combining the three parts of *Henry VI* and *Richard III* is hard to underestimate. In 1937, having seen the plays performed in sequence in America, the scholar R.W. Chambers wrote:

> To see this was to realise that Shakespeare began his career with a tetralogy based on recent history, grim, archaic, crude, yet nevertheless such as, for scope, power, patriotism, and sense of doom, had probably had no parallel since Aeschylus...

Critics have sometimes disparaged this first tetralogy as episodic and amateurish, apprentice work lacking the panache of the later historical dramas. There are various lively scenes, and some characters radiate vitality – in Richard III, Shakespeare (defying historical fact) created a superbly memorable monster, the grotesque and arrogant villain whom audiences love to hate.

Generally, however, characterisation in the first tetralogy tends to be relatively two-dimensional, the verse lacks the later supple expressiveness, and the thematic development is unsubtle. Indeed, the treatment of religious matters is sometimes crudely explicit – as is the related patriotism. What today's critics might term "demonisation of the Other" is almost absurdly blatant. Joan la Pucelle (Jeanne d'Arc), the French leader, for example, is seen to be aided by devils – who eventually desert her although she has offered them her body and soul. On the eve of the Battle of Bosworth, a parade of ghosts curses Richard and blesses his foes.

The Shakespeare of the first tetralogy blithely embarrasses his modern fans by the abundance of jingoistic propaganda. His second tetralogy is much more sophisticated and ambiguous. Indeed, in view of the problems of censorship which he faced, Shakespeare provides remarkably incisive insights into the behaviour of kings and their followers and opponents. The second tetralogy is rich in characterisation, memorable in heroic and plangent rhetoric, crafty in its plotting, and exceptionally intelligent in the way it relates low life to high life, the small to the great, the farcical to the tragic.

The vitality of Shakespeare's second tetralogy has ensured its endurance for more than four centuries, and will probably ensure its endurance for centuries to come. It is not simply a sequence of perennially entertaining plays; it is part of England's cultural identity, and continues to contribute to the shaping of that identity. The tetralogy dramatises nostalgia poignantly and critically; now it, too, forms part of the nation's cultural nostalgia. At the same time, it exposes the continuing wiles of politicians, and offers ever-topical warnings about the cost of military ventures overseas.

What are the main themes of the four plays?

In 1944, E.M.W. Tillyard, in his highly influential study, *Shakespeare's History Plays*, emphasised the thematic coherence of the first tetralogy, and its links with the second. In particular, he argued that Shakespeare, developing the patriotic theme he found in various sources – notably, Hall's Chronicle – showed how the deposition and killing of Richard II had consequences which lasted through the reigns of Henry IV, Henry V, Henry VI, and the wicked Richard III, and culminated in the accession of Henry Tudor as Henry VII.*

According to Tillyard, the hero of the two tetralogies is not any single individual but England itself, the nation, or, as Tillyard sometimes calls it, "Respublica": the nation considered as a commonwealth to which both low and high characters contribute. The climax then comes with the two parts of *Henry IV*. In Tillyard's view, there is a decline in quality in *Henry V* because Shakespeare felt obliged to conform to "the requirements both of the

*Henry Tudor was Queen Elizabeth's grandfather, and, by marrying Elizabeth of York and thus uniting the rival houses of York and Lancaster, he was deemed to have inaugurated a time of peace and unity, a happy outcome after the woes precipitated by the fall of *Richard II*. (That version of events is often called 'the Tudor Myth'.)

chroniclers and of popular tradition" by portraying an ideal monarch who lacks the humanity of his earlier self.

The whole idea of patriotism – what it means and why it's important – lies at the heart of the four plays. Shakespeare eloquently suggests that, under an able ruler who can unite the nation, England can seem specially blessed and powerful. As Simon Schama has said, Shakespeare is helping to engender a patriotic sense of England's unique greatness as a nation – and suggesting the emergence of a "United Kingdom" in which Scotland, Wales and Ireland at last aid England instead of opposing her.

But if Shakespeare suggests England can seem blessed, he also probes that suggestion: for example, although England is, according to Gaunt, this "other Eden, demi-paradise", France is already "the world's best garden" before Henry V's conquest of it. Shakespeare's historical dramas show that repeatedly, alas, England's worst foes have been at home: feuding noblemen have divided and weakened the realm. Even Jack Cade, the anarchistic man of Kent in *Henry VI Part 2*, is merely a pawn of the Duke of York. And the two tetralogies are linked, as we have seen, by a common theme: the terrible consequences of a single act of usurpation.

The second tetralogy, probably written between 1595 and 1599, depicts this act – which brings the

Lancastrians to power – and the resultant turmoil: the plays "define a moral pattern of sin and retribution followed by expiation and success", says Herschel Baker. The last play, *Henry V*, indeed *seems* to be a great success story: the charismatic Henry unites the realm, leads the British to a great victory over the French, and ensures peace by marrying the French princess, Katherine. But then we reach the Epilogue. And its effect is startling. The complete Epilogue, a formally perfect Shakespearian sonnet, is this:

Thus far, with rough and all-unable pen,
Our bending author hath pursued the story,
In little room confining mighty men,
Mangling by starts the full course of their glory.
Small time: but, in that small, most greatly lived
This star of England. Fortune made his sword;
By which the world's best garden he achieved,
And of it left his son imperial lord.
Henry the Sixth, in infant bands crowned King
Of France and England, did this King succeed:
Whose state so many had the managing,
That they lost France, and made his England
bleed:
Which oft our stage has shown; and, for their sake,
In your fair minds let this acceptance take.

After the triumphalism of so much of the final Act, we encounter this utterly subversive ending.

Though the achievements of Henry V were splendid, they were short-lived. We are reminded that he died early, and in the reign of the youthful King Henry VI the gains in France were lost, and England was riven, yet again, by civil war. As the historian Nigel Saul says, it "was in the reign of... Henry VI that the full horror of the curse was to be realised".

Thus, the sense of history as progressive is replaced by the sense of history as cyclical: after civil war, peace, then civil war again; after losses abroad, gains abroad, then losses again. And the cyclical pattern is reflected in the very order of the plays. This elegant sonnet, the epilogue of the final play in the second tetralogy, links the ending of *Henry V* strongly to the opening of *Henry VI Part 1*, the first play in the first tetralogy. Like a vast snake swallowing its tale, the two tetralogies are thus bound together as a cyclical *octology* – an infinite group of eight: a unique theatrical phenomenon.*

A sceptic, looking back over *Henry V* in the

---

*The last words of *Finnegans Wake* begin a sentence completed by that novel's opening words (a positive effect: Vico's cyclical history is being evoked); Samuel Beckett's 1964 drama entitled simply *Play* contains, a few lines from the apparent end, the daunting direction, '*Repeat Play*' (a negative effect: futility is infinitely extended); and fans of Vladimir Nabokov know that in his *Pale Fire*, the final line of its eponymous poem starts a couplet which is completed by that poem's first line (a positive effect: after all, there may be an aesthetic pattern within life's arbitrariness). There are few modern experimentalists whom Shakespeare has not anticipated.

light of that concluding sonnet, might then reflect as follows. The capture of Harfleur, the victory at Agincourt, the marriage to Katherine: it all came to nothing. France was lost and England bled again. The progress of Henry to the throne, and sometimes his conduct as Henry V, may bring to mind the teachings of Niccolò Machiavelli, the Italian political realist who argued that the end justifies the means. Machiavelli was well known to Elizabethans, and was caricatured for them by playwrights as a ruthlessly immoral atheist – he appears on stage in Marlowe's *The Jew of Malta* as the presiding evil genius of the play:

> *I count religion but a childish toy,*
> *And hold there is no sin but ignorance...*
> *Many will talk of title to a crown:*
> *What right had Caesar to the empery?*
> *Might first made kings...*

In *The Prince (Il Principe)*, the authentic Machiavelli declared: "In the affairs of all men, and especially of princes, where there is no tribunal to which we can appeal, we judge by results." That might have been the pragmatic philosophy of Henry IV, too; but, as that King ages, he offers a bleak reading of history:

> *O God, that one might read the book of Fate,*

And see the revolution of the times
Make mountains level, and the continent,
Weary of solid firmness, melt itself
Into the sea...
　　　　　O, if this were seen,
The happiest youth, viewing his progress through,
What perils past, what crosses to ensue,
Would shut the book, and sit him down and die.
　　　　　　　　　[Henry V, III.i]

Here Henry IV resembles a thematic chorus,
eloquently expressing that sense of the futility of
human endeavour which, in the second tetralogy,
intermittently offsets the phases of magniloquence.
But Henry's "book of Fate" is not the only book
before us. The "book of humanity" is there to be
read, too: the book in which we see that Henry IV,
once a reticently ruthless power-seeker, becomes
relatively likeable as he becomes more depressed,
seeing the hollowness of his endeavours.

The ominous sonnet which concludes *Henry V*
makes a confident appeal to its auditors: the cruel
ironies of history, enacted in the theatre, have
provided memorable entertainment "which oft
our stage has shown". The transformative art of
the playwright has, by triumphantly effective
alchemy, rendered the often cruel processes of
history not only comprehensible but enjoyable. In
literary achievements such as this, the pen indeed
seems mightier than the sword.

RICHARD II

A summary of the plot

Act One

Two noblemen, Bolingbroke and Mowbray, quarrel bitterly, each accusing the other of being a traitor. The basis of the quarrel seems to be the question: who was responsible for the murder of Thomas Woodstock, Earl of Gloucester? Richard II urges the quarrelling noblemen to be reconciled. When his advice is not taken, he orders them to trial by combat – but then interrupts that trial to pronounce sentence. Mowbray is banished from England for life. Bolingbroke is sentenced to ten years of exile, soon commuted to six years. Meanwhile, we learn from old John of Gaunt, Bolingbroke's father, that the King himself was guilty of Woodstock's death. (In early texts, 'Bolingbroke' is spelt 'Bullingbrooke'.)*

Act Two

The dying Gaunt, while patriotically praising England as "This other Eden, demi-paradise", reproaches Richard for being a ruler who is ruthlessly and recklessly despoiling the land. On Gaunt's death, Richard declares that he will seize Bolingbroke's inheritance. The Duke of York protests, because the King, by thus breaching the laws of succession and inheritance, is striking at

*All quotations from *Richard II*, *Henry IV Parts 1 and 2*, and *Henry V* are taken from the Wordsworth texts edited by Cedric Watts.

16

the basis of his own authority. (It's symbolically suicidal.) Noblemen – Northumberland, Ross and Willoughby – grumble that the King is "basely led / By flatterers" and is taxing the nobility and the common people alike. Bolingbroke, after his exile, is on his way back to England.

Act Three

Richard goes to Ireland to pursue the war against the rebels there, leaving the Duke of York in charge of the realm. York confronts Bolingbroke but says he lacks the power to arrest him. Bolingbroke affirms that he has returned to claim only his own inheritance, but he also declares that he intends to deal ruthlessly with Richard's favourites, Bushy and Greene: and they are duly executed. Richard returns from Ireland to find that Bolingbroke's insurrection seems too powerful to be overcome, and, while asserting that, as an anointed king, he has divine support, Richard surrenders to Bolingbroke, who renews his assurance that he seeks only his inheritance from Gaunt.

Act Four

At Westminster Hall, Bolingbroke presides over a parliament at which the members quarrel fiercely, the basis of the quarrel being, once again, culpability for the death of Gloucester. The Duke of York enters to say that Richard is willing to adopt Bolingbroke as his heir. "In God's name, I'll ascend the royal throne," responds Bolingbroke. The Bishop of Carlisle prophesies that if Bolingbroke dares to claim the throne, appalling civil war will follow. The Bishop is arrested for treason.

Richard is brought in and, bitterly, waveringly and reluctantly, performs a ritual of abdication. Bolingbroke announces that his own coronation will soon take place. Meanwhile, Carlisle, the Abbot of Westminster and Aumerle are already plotting against him. Richard poignantly parts from his Queen, Isabel. York learns that his son, Aumerle, is part of a plot to dethrone Bolingbroke, and heads for court to denounce Aumerle; but his son reaches Bolingbroke first, and solicits a pardon, which Bolingbroke grants.

Act Five

Richard, brooding at Pomfret (Pontefract) Castle, is assailed and murdered by a gang led by Sir Piers Exton, who believes the deed fulfils Bolingbroke's wish. The conspiracy against Bolingbroke ends: the Abbot of Westminster has died, and Bolingbroke mercifully consigns Carlisle to retirement. Exton presents the corpse of Richard to Bolingbroke, but Bolingbroke responds: "Though I did wish him dead, / I hate the murtherer, love him murtherèd." Furthermore, he adds that he intends to go to the Holy Land to assuage his guilt.

CRITICS ON RICHARD II

"In [Richard's] prosperity we saw him imperious and oppressive, but in his distress he is wise, patient, and pious."

Samuel Johnson (*The Plays of William Shakespeare*, 1765)

"He is weak, variable, and womanish, and possesses feelings which, amiable in a female, are displaced in a man, and altogether unfit for a king... I know of no character drawn by our poet with such unequalled skill as that of Richard II."

Samuel Taylor Coleridge (*Lectures*, 1811-12)

"His folly, his vices, his misfortunes, his reluctance to part with the crown, his fear to keep it, his weak and womanish regrets, his starting tears, his fits of hectic passion, his smothered majesty, pass in succession before us, and make a picture as natural as it is affecting."

William Hazlitt (*Characters of Shakespear's Plays*, 1817)

"Shakespeare... knew instinctively that the preciosity and self-regarding sentiment of Richard could not stand *comic criticism* or even lapse of seriousness."

A.P.Rossiter in *Angel with Horns*, 1951

"When the dying Gaunt puns on his own name, Richard finds this word-play profoundly irritating: "Can sick men play so nicely with their names?" This is pretty rich, coming as it does from a king who seems unable to scratch his nose without making a symbol out of it. As a "poet king", Richard trusts to the sway of the signifier: only by translating unpleasant political realities into decorative verbal fictions can he engage with them... It is not surprising that Richard, like so many politicians, is both callous and sentimental."

Terry Eagleton in *William Shakespeare*, 1986

To what extent is *Richard II* a tragedy?

John Heminge and Henry Condell, when editing the First Folio, divided Shakespeare's plays into comedies, histories and tragedies; this division, proving useful, has been widely adopted. It can also, of course, be misleading. Numerous dramas straddle genres. For instance, *Julius Caesar* and *Antony and Cleopatra*, though categorised in the Folio as tragedies, could as well be counted as histories. *Troilus and Cressida* was termed a history in the first quarto but a tragedy in the First Folio.

Richard II is one of Shakespeare's finest works: lucid and eloquent, thoroughly poetic, strongly and intelligently structured. To a large extent, it shifts and changes according to the observer's viewpoint and the context in which it is observed. The work can be regarded as a tragedy, or a history play, or a political drama, or as one part of a vast dramatic cycle which helped to generate England's national identity. Each time you try it in a different genre, it seems to rotate and burgeon, displaying new aspects of itself.

It was originally registered, in 1597, as *The Tragedye of Richard the Second*; and the first quarto, issued in the same year, was entitled *The Tragedie of King Richard the second*. Just as an individual can be related to two and more families, so can a literary work. If you think of *Richard II* as a history play, questions of factual accuracy and political distortion then come to mind. Think of it as a tragedy, and it will invite comparison with such classical works as *Agamemnon, King Oedipus* and *The Bacchae*. In *Richard II*, as in all three of those ancient plays, we see a ruler who is tainted by arrogance and fecklessly ignores good advice, but, in his downfall, becomes a sympathetic object of concern. The main plot thus displays a familiar pattern of tragic irony.

For Chaucer's monk in *The Canterbury Tales*, a tragedy told a simple exemplary story: that of a person who stood in an eminent position and enjoyed prosperity but who, as the "Wheel of Fortune" turned, fell into misery and ended wretchedly. The moral: put your trust not in this unreliable world but in the prospect of heaven for the virtuous. This was the doctrine of Boethius's *De Consolatione Philosophiae* (*c.* 524 A.D., translated by Chaucer and by Elizabeth I). In 1904, however, A.C.Bradley, in his *Shakespearean Tragedy*, declared that "tragedy would not be tragedy if it were not a painful mystery". There, modern agnosticism seems to have influenced the concept: instead of being morally and theologically specific, tragedy hints at profound mysteries but eschews the didactic.

In the Elizabethan Age, dramatists depicting a

tragic protagonist were pulled between (a) the traditional, Chaucerian sense of the exemplary case, illustrating the turning of Fortune's wheel, and (b) a more modern sense of the value of complexity and ambiguity. In *Richard II*, our view of Richard probably shifts from one of disgust, when he cynically welcomes Gaunt's death, to one of pity or sympathy as he is encompassed by enemies and becomes the introspective victim. Meanwhile, numerous speeches offer us moral and theological interpretations of the events.

Richard II exemplifies a great paradox which is often exploited in the tradition of "regal tragedy". A king may be semi-divine, God's deputy on earth, and (according to the official 16th-century Homilies) judgeable by the Lord alone; but a king is, inevitably, fallible, vulnerable, subject to envy and possibly rebellion, and ultimately mortal. Of course, there could be tragedies about young lovers or a deceived soldier: *Romeo and Juliet* and *Othello* prove that. In regal tragedy, however, the exalted status of the vulnerable monarch serves to magnify greatly the significance of his fate.

It also magnifies the social consequences of a familiar disparity which probably lurks within most of us. This is a disparity between the greater self we can imagine and the humdrum self that we usually inhabit. In a perishable carcass, a mediocre person may harbour exalted and perhaps immortal longings. Arthur Miller's *Death of a Salesman* exemplifies this. When King Richard falls, however, others fall with him, some of them to their deaths. Division within the royal family may entail division – civil war – for the whole country.

Sometimes, for Richard, the sense that he is a mere mortal is dominant, as when he says:

> *I live with bread like you, feel want,*
> *Taste grief, need friends: subjected thus,*
> *How can you say to me, I am a king?*
> *[III.iii]*

At other times, his sense of semi-divinity prevails:

> *Not all the water in the rough rude sea*
> *Can wash the balm from an anointed king.*
> *The breath of worldly men cannot depose*
> *The deputy elected by the Lord.*
> *[III.ii]*

"Yet looks he like a king," remarks York, when Richard stands at bay; and Richard, even as he dies, asserts (in ritualising couplets) his royalty and his heavenly destiny:

> *Exton, thy fierce hand*
> *Hath with the King's blood stained the King's own*
> *land.*
> *Mount, mount, my soul; thy seat is up on high,*

Whilst my gross flesh sinks downward, here to die.
[V.v]

If, in the early part of the play, Richard seems callous, feckless and cynical, it is in his downfall that his consciousness of his role as God's deputy gathers force. The England of *Richard II* was termed by Gaunt "this other Eden", Richard's

THE ROLE OF WOMEN

In the first scene of *Richard II*, Mowbray says:

'Tis not the trial of a woman's war,
The bitter clamour of two eager tongues,
Can arbitrate this cause betwixt us twain.

What ensues is indeed "the bitter clamour of two eager tongues", much rhetoric and no physical combat. The Duchess of Gloucester will reproach Gaunt for being unmanly in not avenging Gloucester's murder. Queen Isabel will rebuke Richard for being willing to "kiss the rod" instead of behaving like a lion. A critic, Margaret Healy, comments that this play

shows us a few competent women locked into roles which forbid them centre-stage parts, and several foolish, vain unreasonable men – including King Richard – inhabiting centric roles they are totally unfit for. The external signs of manhood and womanhood are revealed as frequently misleading – women can belie cultural stereotypes and be intelligent and reasonable, men can behave like babes ■

downfall is "a second Fall of cursèd man", and the monarch even compares himself to the betrayed Christ – though Jesus was betrayed by only one Judas. After Richard's death, his sacred dimension gains increasing warranty. Bolingbroke curses the killer, Exton – "With Cain go wander through the shades of night" [V.vi] – and then promises to undertake a pilgrimage to purge his own guilt:

> I'll make a voyage to the Holy Land,
> To wash this blood off from my guilty hand.
>
> *[V.vi]*

It is a voyage which Henry IV never has the leisure to make, and this is partly because he is beset by political and familial worries. God, it may seem, is avenging the betrayed and murdered Richard. In *The Oresteia*, the fallible Agamemnon grows posthumously in stature: his avenging spirit strikes back. In *Richard II*, the fallible king, when dead, is never gone: his spirit seems to blight the lives of his foes and their descendants.

As in the ancient tragedies of Aeschylus, Sophocles and Euripides, the fate of the tragic protagonist evokes the problem of theodicy: the theological problem of reconciling the fact of human suffering with the notion that the world is governed by a just God or by just gods. Historically, complex tragedy emerges when traditional religious beliefs are challenged by new scepticism: orthodoxies are questioned; perhaps, as C.S.Lewis remarked bitterly in a lecture I attended, "heavenly consolation is no earthly use". Tragedy then aspires to resolve as paradox the conflict between human hope and humiliating fact.

What is the moral dilemma at the heart of Richard II?

Ernest Schanzer once wrote a book on three Shakespearian 'problem plays' (as he termed them): *Julius Caesar*, *Measure for Measure* and *Antony and Cleopatra*. Schanzer said that a problem play has a central moral problem which is presented in such a way that we are uncertain of our moral bearings, "so that uncertain and divided responses to it in the minds of the audience are possible or even probable". In such works, the dramatist may employ "dramatic coquetry", "manipulating our response to the principal characters, playing fast and loose with our affections for them, engaging and alienating them in turn". These were useful notions, but they obviously apply to far more of Shakespeare's plays than the three specified by Schanzer; indeed, any of Shakespeare's works may be "problematised" by a resourceful critic.

Schanzer's definition can, however, be fruitfully applied to *Richard II*. In this play, a "central moral problem" is that of the rebellion: is it justified or not? A related question is "Which ruler is better for the nation: Richard or Bolingbroke?" As for "dramatic coquetry", consider how the play opens.

It may well seem a bewildering opening. When King Richard presides over the dispute between Bolingbroke (the Duke of Hereford) and Thomas Mowbray (the Duke of Norfolk), each duke vehemently accuses the other of treason. Bolingbroke particularly accuses Mowbray of slaying Thomas Woodstock, the Earl of Gloucester, and Mowbray denies this charge, though remarking rather enigmatically that he had "neglected his sworn duty" in that matter. The King hears them out, and urges them to "Forget, forgive, conclude and be agreed" – which seems eminently sensible advice. Many readers and spectators, unable to choose between the bewilderingly assertive rivals, will be inclined to trust the King. The two noblemen continue to quarrel, however, and the King, declaring "We were not born to sue, but to command", orders them to prepare for trial by combat.

In the second scene, we find John of Gaunt arguing with Woodstock's widow, the Duchess of Gloucester. She urges him to take vengeance on the killers of Woodstock. Gaunt responds:

God's is the quarrel; for God's substitute,
His deputy anointed in His sight,
Hath caused his death; the which if wrongfully,
Let heaven revenge, for I may never lift
An angry arm against His minister.
                                    [I.ii]

We are thus surprised – and shocked – to learn
how hypocritical had been Richard's performance
in the previous scene, for Gaunt here tells us that
Richard himself had ordered Woodstock's death.
But Gaunt now shows that he subscribes to the
doctrine that would eventually, in Elizabeth's
reign, be propagated in the "Homily against
Disobedience and Wilful Rebellion", which, read
out in churches, regularly reminded her subjects
of the fate of Adam and Eve, seduced to
disobedience by the rebellious Satan. Subjects
should *never* rebel against a monarch, however
bad he might be; a bad monarch was God's way of
punishing the subjects for their sins, and in due
time God would deal with the malefactor. "Christ
taught us plainly, that even the wicked rulers have
their power and authority from God, and therefore
it is not lawful for subjects to withstand them."
That's what the Homily declared.

   In the third scene, after the preparations for
the duel at Coventry, the King, ostensibly in the
interests of peace, suddenly intervenes to prevent
the combat: he sentences Mowbray to permanent

exile and Bolingbroke to six years' exile. Once again, Richard sounds authoritative and even wise in seeking order and tranquillity in the realm. In the following scene, however, we hear Richard talking to his cronies, Bagot, Greene and Aumerle, and, when Bushy enters to announce that John of Gaunt is "grievous sick", the King's response is thoroughly cynical:

> *Now put it, God, in the physician's mind*
> *To help him to his grave immediately!*
> *The lining of his coffers shall make coats*
> *To deck our soldiers for these Irish wars.*
> *Come, gentlemen, let's all go visit him:*
> *Pray God we may make haste, and come too*
>   *late!*
>
> *ALL: Amen.*
>
>   [I.iv]

Here is "dramatic coquetry" indeed. Prismatically, Richard's character is shown to be complex and deceptive, publicly just, privately cynical. Yet, as the play proceeds and Richard, beset by enemies, loses power and is on a doomed course, he becomes poignantly introspective and self-critical: "I wasted time, and now doth Time waste me" [V.v]. The poignancy is accentuated by vivid details. For instance, the stableman who visits Richard in the prison at Pomfret Castle says that Richard's own horse, a roan Barbary, seemed

29

proud to be ridden by Bolingbroke – so even his horse betrays him. Then there is York's account of Richard's being reviled by the crowds:

> *No joyful tongue gave him his welcome home;*
> *But dust was thrown upon his sacred head,*
> *Which with such gentle sorrow he shook off,*
> *His face still combating with tears and smiles*
> *(The badges of his grief and patience),*
> *That had not God for some strong purpose steeled*
> *The hearts of men, they must perforce have melted,*
> *And barbarism itself have pitied him.*
>
> *[V.ii]*

It's almost sentimental in its blatant appeal for a sympathetic response (and it may briefly bring to mind the arrested Christ's ill-treatment by the Jewish people and the Roman authorities). But John Dryden, in 1679, was one of many critics who responded warmly: "I have scarce read anything comparable to it... Consider the wretchedness of his condition, and his carriage in it; and refrain from pity if you can." As we have noted, Richard dies fighting valiantly, though outnumbered. Even the leading murderer, Exton, deems Richard "as full of valour as of royal blood" [V.v].

It is not only Richard who divides our feelings. Consider York, apparently weak but credibly

Opposite: Richard II (1367-1400). Wood engraving c.1900

pragmatic in supporting the person who seems the most powerful; yet prepared even to sacrifice his son to the new ruler. Again, Bolingbroke initially wins some sympathy, particularly when Richard cuts off his inheritance; but gradually doubts arise: is he a covert Machiavellian? He is ruthless to the favourites, but later his guiltiness makes him treat Aumerle mercifully.

As a whole, the play provides a wide range of insights into politics, particularly into the contrasts between the public panoply, the outward display, and the harsher realities of the manipulations of wealth and power. It reminds us that much of what passes for recorded history is a collection of accounts of human violence, greed, exploitation and stupidity. Fallible mortals claim

SHAKESPEARE'S SOURCES

The main source was the *Chronicles of England, Scotland, and Ireland* by Raphael Holinshed and others, customarily ascribed simply to Holinshed. In

particular, Shakespeare used the 1587 second edition. This provided the main sequence of events to be dramatised; but Shakespeare's poetic rendering gives memorable eloquence, expressive characterisation and descriptive vividness to what Holinshed offers in functional prose.

Holinshed takes the view that Richard, for all his faults – adultery (elided by Shakespeare), extravagance and choosing bad counsellors supernatural authority. The noted figures tend to be the powerful and prominent, rather than the considerate, kind and constructive.

In Act Three, Scene Four, the Queen and her ladies encounter the gardener and his two men. One of the men asks why they should strive to keep everything orderly in their garden when "the sea-walled garden, the whole land" is weedy, disorderly and swarming with caterpillars. Richard has been a bad gardener, letting forms of corruption flourish. This scene has thematic continuity with Gaunt's patriotic "sceptred isle" speech in Act Two, Scene One, which links the pristine England to Eden, and laments that now this "blessed plot" has become a "pelting [paltry] farm". The gardener and his men could teach the

---

– remained a "bountiful and loving" sovereign, a "right noble and worthy prince". Bolingbroke lacked "moderation and loyalty" and showed "tiger-like cruelty"; accordingly, "both he himself and his lineal race were scourged afterwards, as a dire punishment unto rebellious subjects".

Regarding the manner of Richard's death, Holinshed considers three options: (i) that Richard was starved; (ii) that Richard chose to starve himself; and (iii) that he was slain by assassins. Holinshed inclines to the third option, and reports a detailed account of Richard's valiant battle against nine attackers. Shakespeare naturally chose the last option, the most dramatic of them.

Another source was Samuel Daniel's *Civil Wars*. This provided the basis of the poignant parting of Richard (mocked and insulted by the populace) from Isabel, his loyal and loving queen ∎

King a lesson. Indeed, the productive continuities of rural life are made to comment critically on the turbulence of the world of power politics.

This theme will extend into *Henry IV Part 2* and the Gloucestershire scenes, and will have an ironic coda when the Epilogue of *Henry V* tells us that the King gained "the world's best garden" – France – but it was soon lost. The Queen protests that the gardeners are prying into mysteries of state; the fact that their utterance is in blank verse rather than prose gives them an incursionary dignity; and David Norbrook suggests that here

> *Richard II* contains an oblique prophecy of its own censorship: the play is aware that it is touching on sensitive areas of political discourse, areas that displace a top-down hierarchy.

The play hints at the possibility that the anonymous gardener and the groom have done more good than have Richard and Bolingbroke.

Repeatedly, in the tradition of the problem play, this drama questions matters that might at first appear straightforward, making them fruitfully problematic. It may remind us that Bertolt Brecht, the Marxist dramatist, followed the lead of Henrik Ibsen and George Bernard Shaw by claiming that his dramas had the function of making the audience think about problematic matters (before coming to the Marxist conclusion which the Brechtian play solicited). Brecht was strongly influenced by Elizabethan drama. Shakespeare showed Brecht the way forward.

Editors Jonathan Dawson and Eric Yachnin claim that in *Richard II* Shakespeare, unlike Holinshed, is conservative in using the noun "subjects" rather than "citizens", but, emphasising the Elizabethan theatre as a new forum for public debate, they declare that *Richard II*

> is radical, but not primarily because of its ideological content, much of which is in any case deeply conservative. It is radical because of its cultivation of the public practices of discussing, debating, and judging among ordinary people.

Nevertheless, "deeply conservative" is not how Queen Elizabeth regarded it.

What is so special about the language of *Richard II*?

When Mowbray is attempting to vindicate himself before King Richard, he says:

> *My dear dear lord:*
> *The purest treasure mortal times afford*
> *Is spotless reputation: that away,*
> *Men are but gilded loam or painted clay.*
> *A jewel in a ten-times barred-up chest*
> *Is a bold spirit in a loyal breast.*
> *Mine honour is my life; both grow in one:*
> *Take honour from me, and my life is done.*
> > *[I.i]*

This speech introduces the theme of honour, its nature and value, which will resound throughout the tetralogy. Mowbray's utterance here is memorably eloquent, but obviously it is lyrically poetic, rather than realistic. *Richard II* is a remarkably lyrical history play. It is written almost entirely in verse – iambic pentameter – and much of that verse rhymes in "heroic couplets", as in that speech by Mowbray. This helps to create subliminally the impression that the world of *Richard II* is a now-bygone world in which ceremony and formalism went hand in hand with traditional order, even though that order was being subverted, initially by the monarch himself. Herschel Baker says:

> Richard is such a virtuoso in the arts of speech that when he fondles words and tropes he seems to listen to himself, tuning his language not merely to his situation but also to his mood, and rejoicing in his skill.

Baker notes that Richard can proceed

> within the compass of a single scene (III.ii) to the soft, caressing music of his salutation to the English earth, the deep-toned splendour of his hymn to royal power, the cacophony of his diatribe on the "three Judases", and finally to his lovely song about the death of kings.

He becomes a man who prefers to reflect and verbalise rather than to act, whereas Bolingbroke never lets words take the place of action. Bolingbroke says:

> *O, who can hold a fire in his hand*
> *By thinking on the frosty Caucasus?*
> *[I.iii]*

Richard is fascinated by symbolism; Bolingbroke is irritated by it. When, in the deposition scene, Richard smashes the mirror, he says to Bolingbroke:

Mark, silent King, the moral of this sport:
How soon my sorrow hath destroyed my face.

[IV.i]

At this, the "silent King" speaks, and it is with curtly deflationary precision:

The shadow of your sorrow hath destroyed
The shadow of your face.

In other words: "You are talking nonsense. In fact, your performance of sorrow has destroyed merely

CENSORSHIP AND *RICHARD II*

Richard II, says Ralph Berry, was once "the most dangerous, the most politically vibrant play in the canon". Obviously, it has dangerous subject-matter: it depicts a successful rebellion against an anointed monarch, who is then killed. The

deposition scene (Act Four, Scene One) was doubtless enacted on stage, being so important; but most of it was omitted from the first, second and third quartos, for obvious political reasons.

The scene shows parliament taking precedence over the king. The depiction of a rightful English monarch forced to hand over the crown to a usurper would have been offensive to Queen Elizabeth and her censorious representatives. Phyllis Rackin, in *The Stages of History*, says: "Janus-faced, the image of your face." Richard is nonplussed: "Say that again."

In the following plays, *Henry IV Parts 1 and 2*, there will be less poetry, markedly less rhyme, and markedly more prose. In *Henry IV Part 1*, about 45 per cent of the text is prose (and Falstaff has more lines than anyone else). In *Henry IV Part 2*, about 50 per cent is prose (and Falstaff has far more lines than anyone else). The result is a greater range of expressiveness and a more realistic treatment of characterisation. It seems that after the downfall of Richard we have moved into a fallen world: a more modern, familiar world.

We see ceremony starting to break down even

---

the history of *Richard II* looks backward to a lost medieval past, but also looks forward to a disquieting Elizabethan present."

The once-popular Earl of Essex had fallen out of royal favour after the failure of his military campaign against rebels in Ireland. Subsequently, in collaboration with the Earl of Southampton, he plotted an insurrection. On February 7th, 1601, his supporters paid Shakespeare's company 40 shillings (to complement box-office takings) for a special production of *Richard II* at the Globe Theatre, evidently because they thought the play would serve as a kind of rallying-cry.

Elizabeth I was later reported to have said, evidently in anger: "I am Richard II, know ye not that?" She complained that the downfall of Richard II was enacted "forty times in open streets and houses". Her remark shows that Elizabethans were quick to see the contemporary political implications of literary works about the historical past. She also knew that Catholic polemicists within *Richard II*. After Bolingbroke gains power, the dissension among the noblemen in Act Four, Scene One – again dissension prompted largely by the matter of Woodstock's death – is very disorderly compared with the ritualised dissension of Act One. Later, when the Duke and Duchess of York petition Henry IV, he says:

> *Our scene is altered from a serious thing,*
> *And now changed to "The Beggar and the King".*
>   *[V.iii]*

were currently claiming that it was a Christian duty to assassinate the Protestant Queen.

Obviously, Elizabethans saw analogies between the rule of Elizabeth and that of Richard: neither monarch had a direct heir; both were criticised for favouritism and heavy taxation – farming the realm.

Richard II depicts the ordinary people as fickle, easily swayed to follow first one leader and then another. (This notion is exploited in numerous plays by Shakespeare, notably the *Henry VI* trilogy and *Julius Caesar*.) In reality, however, when Essex and his men made their insurrectionary passage through London, the citizens, instead of impulsively following the Earl, took note but prudently stayed aloof. The insurrection failed; the once-popular Earl himself was sentenced to death for high treason, and executed. His supporter, the Earl of Southampton (Shakespeare's patron and probably the "lovely boy" of the sonnets), was also sentenced to death, but his sentence was commuted to life imprisonment. At the trial, Sir Edward Coke opined that Elizabeth would not have lived long, had she fallen into Essex's clutches, adding: "how long lived Richard the Second after he was surprised in the same manner?"

He notes that familial disorder is subverting the decorum of the court, but – this being the play *Richard II* – even Henry's observation takes the form of a rhyming couplet. The pervasive verse of *Richard II* lends a sheen of medievalism to events. In contrast, the tavern scenes of *Henry IV Part 1*, though supposedly set in the early 15th century, abound in the colloquial prose of Shakespeare's day.

The Privy Council called in one of the shareholders of Shakespeare's company, Augustine Phillips, to explain what the players thought they were doing in staging the play on that occasion. His explanation, that the company were persuaded by the forty shillings, implying political innocence, was evidently found satisfactory, for the Chamberlain's Men continued to enjoy generous patronage from the royal court.

Incidentally, Essex's great rival at court had been Sir Walter Raleigh; and Sir Walter was sentenced to the Tower of London in 1603 and executed in 1618. One obvious theme of *Richard II* – that nobody, however great, is immune to the turning of Fortune's wheel – had plenty of illustrations in Shakespeare's era.

The deposition scene of *Richard II* was restored, in rather mangled form, in the fourth quarto (1608), which proudly declared that it contained "new additions of the Parliament Sceane, and the deposing of King Richard"; it remained in the fifth quarto (1615) and was present in the First Folio. Evidently, when Elizabeth's heir, James VI of Scotland, since 1603 James I of Great Britain, was safely enthroned, the deposition scene was no longer deemed so risky ∎

REWRITING HISTORY

Richard II, born on 6 January 1367, reigned from 1377 until his deposition in 1399 and died in captivity early in 1400. He was the last king since William the Conqueror to rule by undisputed hereditary right, *de jure* (rightfully, lawfully). In the following century, kings were *de facto* – in practice but not by right.

Richard had no children. He had declared (it was widely believed) that the heir to his throne was Roger Mortimer, the fourth Earl of March, who, via his mother, was descended from Edward III. The fourth Earl died in battle in 1398, so the heir was then his son, Edmund, the fifth Earl.* At the time of Richard's death, the heir-designate was seven years old.

Lancastrian propaganda claimed that Richard had voluntarily abdicated his throne to the martial victor, Bolingbroke. Shakespeare dramatises Richard's poignant situation in the deposition scene; in reality, there was no such confrontation. In Richard's absence, a deed of abdication was read out, as were 33 charges against him. Henry of Lancaster then claimed the throne by descent, conquest, and the need for better rule.

*Shakespeare, like Holinshed, confused him with his uncle, another Edmund Mortimer, who married the daughter of the Welsh rebel Glendower.

The claim by descent was based on the fact that though Bolingbroke's father, John of Gaunt, was a younger son of Edward III than was Lionel, Duke of Clarence, from whom the Earls of March claimed descent, the Earls of March inherited via the female line, through Lionel's daughter Philippa, whereas Bolingbroke's descent was via the male, John of Gaunt. But the English monarchy did not disqualify inheritance via the female line, and, indeed, Henry V would later approve the female line when seeking to vindicate his claim to the French throne. The historian A.R.Myers says of Bolingbroke's ascent:

> The fact was that a great magnate had taken advantage of discontent to seize the throne by force. His title by descent was weak, and the claim to make a revolution because of "default of governance and undoing of the good laws" was a weapon which could later be used against him.

As was his custom, Shakespeare took considerable liberties with the historical facts. In *Richard II*, he compressed the lengthy time-scale and ignored many important events, such as the Peasants' Revolt, which took place between Richard's coronation and 1397.

In the play, a poignant character is Richard's Queen, Isabel. She appears in three scenes, a worried, devoted, loving and spirited wife. In Act Five, Scene One, her parting from Richard is movingly protracted, modulating from the relatively realistic, as she urges him to show more courage and defiance, to the lyrically stylised, as their last loving farewell becomes a duet in rhyming couplets. The real Queen, however, was no woman but a child. She was born on November 9th, 1389, he on January 6th, 1367. Therefore, at the time of their marriage by proxy on March 12th, 1396, Richard was 29 and Isabel was six; at his deposition in 1399, he was 33 and she ten.

In that era, it was not unusual for political and dynastic considerations to result in matches which had similar disparities in ages. To increase dramatic tension, human interest and political reflections, Shakespeare often departs from the reports in the chronicles. Obviously, he has thus given the plight of Richard and his Queen a poignancy which it would otherwise have lacked.

Here's another instance of Shakespeare's freedom in adaptation. Shakespeare's John of Gaunt is famously a romantic patriot, who, in an invented scene, extols the splendour of England – "This royal throne of kings, this sceptred isle" – and denounces the misrule by Richard. You wouldn't guess from the play that the historic John of Gaunt was a highly unpopular magnate who, when he gained the upper hand in Edward III's parliament in 1376-77, headed a coalition containing corrupt household servants, courtiers and officials. During the Peasants' Revolt (1381), the rebels destroyed his palace, the Savoy, in London. Shakespeare chooses to idealise his Gaunt, giving him a powerfully choric function, echoed by that remarkably knowledgeable and homiletic gardener (obviously an invented character) in Act Two, Scene Four.

As for the way Richard's reign comes to an end: Shakespeare's play shows a king who submits to Bolingbroke and reluctantly agrees to abdicate, but the play makes clear that this does not validate Bolingbroke's claim to the throne: Bolingbroke evinces guilt and, as Henry IV, admits that he gained the throne by "by-paths and indirect crook'd ways" [IV.v]. Shakespeare's Henry V and even Henry VI will confess privately that their claim to the throne is weak.

The historical facts concerning Richard's arrest and deposition appear to be that Richard, deceived by Bolingbroke (who had sworn that he had no designs on the throne), was treacherously ambushed and captured by forces loyal to the usurper, and thereafter kept prisoner until his death. Richard did not abdicate in person before a full audience in the Palace of Westminster. He remained imprisoned, while the assembly (before an empty throne) heard the reading of a document of abdication which Richard was said to have signed.

Previously in the play, violence has repeatedly been averted; in the final Act, it at last erupts – in the theatre it's therefore all the more effective. Richard valiantly kills two of his numerous assailants before being slain himself. Certainly, one of the early chroniclers (the author of the *La Traïson et Mort de Richard II*) stated that Richard was hacked to death, on Bolingbroke's orders, by a gang of eight led by Exton. This story was favoured by Holinshed. Centuries later, however, when Richard's skeleton was exhumed, it bore no marks of violence. Modern historians therefore give more credence to the other versions offered by chroniclers. Writers supporting the Lancastrian cause say (rather implausibly) that Richard died of a combination of grief and self-starvation. Another suggestion is that he was smothered.

The most likely option is that Richard was deliberately starved by his captors. Clearly, Shakespeare's choice gives the play a more dramatic climax and, again, helps to win sympathy for Richard by showing that though formerly, when in adversity, he was inclined to reflect rather than act, in this final desperate emergency he can act with pride, courage and effectiveness.

A recent historian, Nigel Saul, claims that though Shakespeare took liberties with the facts, he captured the essence of Richard's character. Saul says:

Shakespeare saw… the very essence of Richard's tragedy: that Richard, though unkinged, was still kingly. This powerful insight, the fruit of Shakespeare's fascination with Richard, affords a clue to the many difficulties that he experienced as a ruler... Richard... saw attacks on his kingship as attacks on his own personality... All the most vital aspects of Richard's being – his intense self-regard, his craving for attention, his taste for the theatrical, his appetite for grandeur, and at the same time his greatest weakness, his inner emptiness – find a place in [Shakespeare's] reading. Shakespeare offered the insights of a dramatist and not a historian. But his characterisation of the king and his understanding of what mattered to him probably bring us closer to the historical figure than many a work of history... Perhaps the actor in Shakespeare responded to the actor in Richard. Certainly in the theatre of medieval monarchy there was no keener actor than Richard. His tragedy was that he mistook the illusion of the stage for the reality of the world around him.

Saul's words make a fine vindication of Shakespeare – and perhaps of the Aristotle who, in *Poetics*, deemed poetry more philosophical and of higher value than history.

How does *Richard II* foreshadow the plays which follow it?

Within *Richard II*, there are obvious signs that Shakespeare was looking ahead to likely sequels. For instance, Harry Percy ("Hotspur"), Northumberland's son, appears in Act Two, Scene Three, and is introduced at some length to Bolingbroke, whom he promises to serve loyally. Given that Hotspur has no important role in *Richard II*, the detailed introduction may seem superfluous, but in the next play, *Henry IV Part 1*, he will figure prominently. Ironically, he will be the most valiant of the rebels defying the new king. Again, before the end of *Richard II*, we hear the new ruler expressing domestic worries – in particular, his fear that his own son is proving both dissolute and disloyal:

> *Can no man tell me of my unthrifty son?*
> *'Tis full three months since I did see him last.*
> *If any plague hang over us, 'tis he.*
>
> *[V.iii]*

The son in question does not appear personally in *Richard II*, but this speech serves as a prelude to *Henry IV Parts 1 and 2*, in which we will be shown extensively the life that this son, Hal, is leading

among such "unrestrainèd loose companions"
as Falstaff and Poins. Bolingbroke remarks
in *Richard II* that he perceives in Hal "some
sparks of better hope, which elder years / May
happily bring forth" [V.iii]; and these words
portend the gradual emergence, in *Henry IV Parts
1 and 2*, of Hal as a truly valiant and noble heir
to the throne, the "better hope" being fulfilled in
Henry V.

The combination of the detailed introduction
of Hotspur and the expression of paternal fears
about Hal's character shows that, before *Richard
II* was completed, Shakespeare was already
thinking ahead to a work in which much of the
interest would depend on the character-contrast
between two Harries: Harry Percy (Hotspur) and
Harry Monmouth (Hal).

In fact, Hotspur was more than 20 years older
than Hal, but Shakespeare chooses to suggest they
are both similarly youthful, inviting us to see them
as comparable and contrasting young rivals for
power. Indeed, in *Henry IV Part 1* the King even
expresses the wish that when both were in the
cradle, some fairy could have exchanged Hotspur
for his Hal, and later says that Hotspur is "no
more in debt to years" than is Hal. This sense
that they are equal in age further strengthens
the network of comparisons which helps to unite
the second tetralogy.

In *Richard II*, we hear various grim prophecies

that the downfall of Richard will inevitably bring divine wrath on the head of the usurper. Both the Bishop of Carlisle and Richard himself offer predictions that if Bolingbroke takes the throne, his reign will be an era of appalling and extensive civil war. In the subsequent two plays, we see that these prophecies are amply fulfilled. Furthermore, their fulfilment is systematically emphasised by Shakespeare. In Act Five, Scene One of *Richard II*, Richard tells the Earl of Northumberland:

> *Northumberland, thou ladder wherewithal*
> *The mounting Bullingbrooke ascends my throne,*
> *The time shall not be many hours of age*
> *More than it is, ere foul sin, gathering head,*
> *Shall break into corruption. Thou shalt think,*
> *Though he divide the realm and give thee half,*
> *It is too little, helping him to all.*

In *Henry IV Part 1*, the prophecy is vindicated: we see that Northumberland, who had helped Bolingbroke to power, is now conspiring against him; and in *Henry IV Part 2*, as the conspiracy continues, Bolingbroke, now King Henry, actually quotes (closely though not exactly) Richard's words:

> *But which of you was by –*
> *[to Warwick:] You, cousin Nevil, as I may*
> *remember –*

When Richard, with his eye brimful of tears,
Then checked and rated by Northumberland,
Did speak these words, now proved a prophecy?
"Northumberland, thou ladder by the which
My cousin Bullingbrooke ascends my throne,"
(Though then, God knows, I had no such intent...),
"The time shall come" – thus did he follow it –
"The time will come, that foul sin, gathering head,
Shall break into corruption" – so went on,
Foretelling this same time's condition,
And the division of our amity.   *[III.i]*

Thus, any interpretation of *Richard II* should be aided by the subsequent works. Since Richard's prophecies are fulfilled, his stature is enhanced, and we may gain the impression that, though he was abundantly fallible as a man, he still retained the sanctity conferred on him by his office as the rightful and consecrated King of England. When in power, he was a poor predictor, and his faith in divine aid (e.g. the angels that should fight Bolingbroke's troops) seemed naive; when out of power, he is eventually vindicated as prophet, and divine wrath seems to be visited on the usurpers. This is the metaphysical irony of Richard II.

A related theme is inaugurated by Bolingbroke's vow to make a penitential pilgrimage to the Holy Land. He is so beset by rebellions that he is unable to undertake the voyage. Near the end of *Henry IV Part 2*, he suffers a fatal stroke and, dying, enquires the name of the chamber in which he was afflicted. The chamber, he is told, is called "Jerusalem". He responds:

> *Laud be to God! Even there my life must end.*
> *It hath been prophesied to me, many years,*
> *I should not die but in Jerusalem,*
> *Which vainly I supposed the Holy Land.*
> *But bear me to that chamber; there I'll lie;*
> *In that Jerusalem shall Harry die.*
>
> *[IV.v]*

So the reference to "the Holy Land" in the closing lines of *Richard II* gains, with hindsight, a strongly ironic resonance.

Such connections enrich the second tetralogy. Consider, for example, the way in which the theme of "the sleepless monarch" is sounded. Although apoplexy may be the immediate cause of Henry's death, *Henry IV Part 2* gives the impression that he is driven to death mainly by sheer weariness induced by the cares of state, and in particular by his worries as he contends with rebellion after rebellion. As the rebels point out, it was he who set their example: in usurping the throne of a king, he has created a precedent for others. Henry IV endures sleepless nights, envying the slumbers enjoyed by humble subjects. In a speech which sheds light on his earlier motives, he confesses to his son that

> *God knows...*
> *By what by-paths and indirect crook'd ways*
> *I met this crown; and I myself know well*
> *How troublesome it sat upon my head.*
>
> *[IV.iii]*

In *Henry V*, we see that the son, too, is a sleepless worried monarch who envies the slumbers of the humble. In both plays, the wakefulness induced by cares of state is linked to guilt at the deposition of Richard. Henry V may seem to be a splendidly successful monarch, uniting Scots, Irish, Welsh and English beneath his banner when he goes abroad to fight the French; but, on the eve of the Battle of Agincourt, after walking among the troops, he reflects bitterly on the guilt he has inherited with the ill-gotten throne:

> *Not today, O Lord,*
> *O not today, think not upon the fault*
> *My father made in compassing the crown.*
> *I Richard's body have interrèd new,*
> *And on it have bestowed more contrite tears*
> *Than from it issued forcèd drops of blood...*
> *More will I do;*
> *Though all that I can do is nothing worth,*
> *Since that my penitence comes after all,*
> *Imploring pardon.*
>
> *[IV.i]*

In the event, it appears that God does, at last, decide to grant that pardon. At the Battle of Agincourt, the English army gains an apparently miraculous victory over the far more numerous French forces. "O God, thy arm was here," says the grateful Henry V. But a protracted bloody era has preceded the successful outcome.

Richard has cast a long and ominous shadow over the usurpers. It could be said, indeed, that Shakespeare's story of Richard is not completed until Act Five of *Henry V*; perhaps not even then. The Christian paradox of the Fortunate Fall is recalled in this second tetralogy. The Fall of Man was bad but led to good. The rebellion against Richard was bad and provoked wrath, but in the long term it was also good, for it led to the eventual successes of Henry V. Devout Christians, particularly if they are English rather than French, may feel that Shakespeare is emphasising the truth, which is that God presides providentially over historical processes.

Sceptics, in contrast, may feel that Shakespeare, reflecting the values of his times, is providing a patriotic falsification of history by suggesting that English political ambitions are fulfilling a supernatural masterplan. Nevertheless, the Chorus which concludes *Henry V* should be remembered – the Chorus foretelling the wretched reign of Henry VI, when France was lost and England bled.

The apparently triumphant closure near the end of *Henry V* is thus subverted rather than qualified. This final Chorus undermines that sense of a progressive evolution from the age of Richard II, and it introduces that daunting suggestion that history is cyclical: after civil war, civil peace, but then civil war again; after usurpation, orderly succession, but then further usurpation. These eight plays (from *Henry VI Part 1* to *Henry V*) certainly helped to generate a sense of English national identity, and some of their great patriotic speeches resonate superbly to this day; but the plays also testify to the appalling cost in human lives exacted over the centuries by political ambition and ideological intolerance.

Richard II is a brilliant fictional history with a tentacular grip on sombre historical realities.

Overleaf: The Cobbe Portrait, *believed to be a life portrait of William Shakespeare (1564–1616), c.1610*

HENRY IV
PART 1

A summary of the plot

Act One

Bolingbroke, now King Henry IV, tells noblemen that the crusade to the Holy Land must be postponed, as rebellions at home must be dealt with. In Wales, Lord Mortimer's forces have been defeated by Owen Glendower and his Welsh army; Mortimer is a captive. On the other hand, in Northumberland, Scottish rebels led by Douglas have been defeated by the forces of Harry Percy, "Hotspur". The King, noting that "riot and dishonour stain the brow" of his son, wishes his son could have been exchanged for Hotspur. Later, Henry complains that Mortimer is a traitor, for he has married Glendower's daughter, and he demands that Hotspur deliver all his prisoners to the King. Subsequently, Worcester and Northumberland tell Hotspur that Richard II had proclaimed Mortimer his heir. Hotspur readily joins Northumberland and Warwick in their planned revolt against Henry IV.

Act Two

Meanwhile, Hal has been amusing himself with Falstaff and his cronies, though he privately declares that this involvement with them will only be temporary, and that his eventual public "reformation" will be the more impressive. At Gad's Hill, Falstaff, Gadshill and Bardolph rob

two travellers, but they are robbed in return by
the disguised Hal and Poins. Later, at a tavern,
Falstaff tells the Prince and Poins how he had
bravely fought many men before having to
relinquish the loot. Hal denounces him as a liar,
but Falstaff claims that he had recognised the
disguised Hal and had therefore spared him:
"Was it for me to kill the heir-apparent?"

Act Three

At Bangor, leading conspirators meet: Glendower,
Worcester, Hotspur and Mortimer. In London,
the King reproaches Hal for his feckless ways,
but Hal persuades his father of his loyalty.

Act Four

The Battle of Shrewsbury impends. On the way
to it, Falstaff tells us that he has "misused the
King's press damnably" by letting able men buy
themselves out, so that his soldiers are mere
"scarecrows".

Act Five

At Shrewsbury, the King offers the rebel leaders
the chance of making peace, but Worcester and
Vernon do not report this offer to their fellow-
rebels, and battle ensues. Hal rescues his father
from Douglas; Douglas fights Falstaff, who
shams death; and Hal fights and slays Hotspur.
Afterwards, Falstaff claims to have slain Hotspur

himself. The battle ends in victory for the King's forces; Douglas has been captured; Worcester and Vernon, also captives, are sentenced to death. Further rebels must now be assailed, notably those led by Northumberland and Glendower.

What makes *Henry IV Part 1* so effective?

In the political field, Hal is preparing for the confrontation with Hotspur; in the personal field, he is relishing – but trying to maintain a critical distance from – the disgraceful charms of the wily Falstaff.

The rebels are picturesquely diversified, ranging from the dour and doughty Scot, Douglas, to Glendower, the bizarrely charismatic Welsh prince who claims supernatural powers, and, of course, the glamorous, bold and impetuous Hotspur, who hubristically declares:

> *By heaven, methinks it were an easy leap*
> *To pluck bright honour from the pale-faced moon.*
> *[I.iii]*

The drama, complex but tightly knit by its network of themes, comparisons and ironies, moves towards the multiple climax: the reconciliation of Hal with his worried father, the defeat of the rebels by the King's forces, the slaying of Hotspur by Hal, and the survival of the cowardly but resourceful Falstaff.

The oscillation between scenes of high politics and low life lends variety and richness. "A persistent duality is the basic principle of organisation," says Herschel Baker, arguing that this structural duality reveals itself through the artful alternation of politics and folly:

> Shuttling from scenes of state and grave affairs to scenes of bawdy wit and dissipation, Shakespeare weaves a rich design where each detail is set against its complementary and contrasting opposite so that they may sharpen one another. In the grouping of the characters the same device is seen.

In its exuberant vitality, its thematic richness and subtlety, in its co-ordination of small details with big matters, and in its keenly intelligent ironies, *Henry IV Part 1* is arguably the most sophisticated literary work since *The Oresteia*. The searching virtuosity is everywhere apparent: in the characterisation, for instance, Falstaff, Glendower, Hotspur, the King and Hal come distinctively to life, and even such minor characters as Francis and Gadshill are strongly individuated.

In modes of vocal eloquence, Shakespeare

seems to be seeking diverse challenges and rising to them, whether it's the martial rhetoric of Hotspur, the Welsh pride of Glendower, the malapropisms of the hostess, Vernon praising the Hal who could "rise from the ground like feathered Mercury"[IV.i], or Falstaff abusing Hal as "you eel-skin, you dried neat's-tongue, you bull's-pizzle, you stockfish" [II.iv]. Hal takes pride in being a master of different modes of discourse, whether it be the brusque style of Hotspur or the jargon of the waiters at the tavern: he regards power achieved by discourse as superior to power gained by force. And his mastery of discourse is

FALSTAFF'S NAME

Henry IV Part 1 seems to have been remarkably popular, for it had seven quarto editions between 1598 and 1622 before publication of the First Folio. This popularity has been ascribed to the presence of Falstaff. But his very name is a consequence of censorship.

Originally, Shakespeare called the character 'Oldcastle'. The historical Sir John Oldcastle, Lord Cobham, had served Henry IV in Scotland, Wales and France, but had become a religious reformer, a Lollard leader (or early Protestant). In 1414 he led a revolt against Henry V, was captured, and was executed as a heretical rebel.

Elizabethan descendants of Oldcastle's widow were Sir William Brooke (seventh of course surpassed by Shakespeare's, for Shakespeare is generating Hal's: a democratic intimation.

Wherever we look in this play, Shakespeare is delivering more than we expect, and delivering with ease, gusto and urbane dexterity. Like Beethoven in his fifth symphony or Welles in *Citizen Kane*, Shakespeare in *Henry IV Part 1* is revelling in achieved mastery. If intelligence is the art of seeing or making connections between apparently unconnected entities, Shakespeare here displays a commanding intelligence.

Lord Cobham) and his son Sir Henry Brooke (eighth Lord Cobham). Evidently they objected to Shakespeare's conferral of their ancestor's name on a dissolute character. Furthermore, from 1596 to 1597 the seventh Lord Cobham was the Lord Chamberlain, overseeing the office of the Master of the Revels and the licensing of plays. Sir Henry Brooke was a friend of Sir Walter Raleigh and an adversary of the faction headed by the Earl of Essex and the Earl of Southampton. Shakespeare, patronised by Southampton, seems to have been tempted to mock the Oldcastle family. However, he evidently was warned off this course, and changed the name.

Traces remain, however. In *Henry IV Part 1*, Falstaff is referred to as "my old lad of the castle" (II.i); in *Henry IV Part 2*, a prefix for a speech by Falstaff is *"Old."*, abbreviating *"Oldcastle"*; and in the Epilogue the speaker, predicting Falstaff's death "of a sweat", prudently adds: "Oldcastle died a martyr, and this is not the man." ∎

What is *Henry IV Part 1* about?

Henry IV Part 1 is about the dubious, double-edged rewards of winning power, and the human price of political success. Bolingbroke, now Henry IV, is a usurper. He has won power dishonourably. He cannot rest content with his achievement in gaining the throne, for he is repeatedly beset by rebels; furthermore, he fears rebellion at home, thinking that his own son, Hal, may desire his death; he even sees Hal as a second Richard, ambling "with shallow jesters and rash bavin wits"[III.ii].

In this febrile atmosphere, betrayal is always in the air. The rebels (in I.iii) think that the King will treacherously seek the deaths of those who helped him to gain power. The King fears that Hal wishes him dead and may "take Percy's pay", being Henry's "nearest and dearest enemy". Gadshill, as the travellers suspect, is treacherous to the law-abiding. Hal and Poins betray Falstaff at Gad's Hill. Northumberland lets down his allies. Hal coaxes Francis to betray his master. Glendower and Mortimer fail to back their fellow-rebels. Worcester and Vernon behave treacherously to their confederates. Falstaff is treacherous to his recruits, leading them "where they are peppered" [V.iii] so that "there's not three of my hundred-and-fifty left alive" (and he'll collect the pay of the dead). When Hal urgently needs a weapon, Falstaff won't lend him a sword, but offers only the contents of his pistol-holster – a bottle of sack.

The lack of trust in this power-obsessed world is evident even within families. Henry IV, as we have seen, distrusts Hal; Northumberland betrays Hotspur, his son; Lady Percy claims that Hotspur's martial ambitions make him maritally unfaithful. Edmund Mortimer, brother of Lady Percy and a relative of Henry IV, joins the rebels, marrying Glendower's daughter. Glendower eventually fails Hotspur.

The reality of power, Shakespeare suggests, is that it depends less on honour (derided by Falstaff as "a word... Air" [V.i]) than on acting skills. Mimicry offers a means to mastery: often it implies knowledge and understanding linked to critical judgement, even mockery. Hotspur mimics a foppish courtier. A starling, says Hotspur, will be taught to mimic Hotspur shouting 'Mortimer!' at the King. In the superb tavern scene (II.iv), Hal mimics Hotspur; Falstaff mimics Henry IV and later Hal; Hal plays Hal and then Henry IV. In the climactic battle, numerous noblemen pretend to be the King, to protect him. Falstaff (after imitating a corpse) acts the part of a bold warrior who has slain Hotspur.

The comparisons the characters make in the play – true, comic, and false – reinforce the theme of disguise. With power so dependent on clever acting, judging accurately is not easy. The King compares Hal to Hotspur, and deems Hotspur a better heir to the throne; he compares Hal with Richard, and decides that Hal shares Richard's follies; Hal compares himself to Hotspur, and decides that his own methods (entailing knowledge of others) are superior to Hotspur's forthright militancy; Falstaff likens the hostess to an otter (as "a man knows not where to have her" [III.iii]) and Bardolph's red face to a *memento mori*, a reminder of hellfires; Vernon likens Hal to "feathered Mercury", swift and agile; in battle, Douglas compares the King to his imitators, and decides that this may be the real monarch after all; Falstaff compares honour to a surgeon, and concludes that honour "hath no skill in surgery" [V.i].

Finally, the play emphasises the toll that political single-mindedness takes on loving relationships. Hotspur's wife reproaches him; Mortimer's wife, weeping, would "be a soldier too, she'll to the wars" [III.i]; Falstaff's claim to Hal's love is rebuffed; the King fears that his son, far from loving him, ambitiously seeks his death.

How Machiavellian is Hal?

Jonathan Bate and Eric Rasmussen, in the introduction to their edition of the play, say:

> Hal can be played equally persuasively as a young man going on a journey towards maturity but still enjoying his departures from the straight and narrow path, or as one of Shakespeare's machiavellian manipulators – energetic and intellectually astute, a brilliant actor but intensely self-conscious, emotionally reined in.

Schanzer's notion of "dramatic coquetry" (see page 26) is again relevant. Bate and Rasmussen suggest that their paradox can be resolved by postulating a Hal who is a "good Machiavel": a political realist who is prepared to be ruthless but who has good aims; he hopes to serve God and his nation.

In *Henry IV Part 1*, Shakespeare delights in the variegated: in characters who are not black or white, but so mixed that judgement repeatedly has to be qualified. Falstaff, the King, the rebels: repeatedly we find that the appealing jostles the repellent, or the attractive tugs against the dangerous. Again, there are scenes which are variegated in the sense that the serious haunts the comic – as in the play-acting scene (II.iv) – or the comic is close to the serious, as when Hotspur teases Glendower almost to a duel (III.i).

Hal's first soliloquy invites a subtly variegated response.

> *I know you all, and will a while uphold*
> *The unyoked humour of your idleness.*
> *Yet herein will I imitate the sun,*
> *Who doth permit the base contagious clouds*
> *To smother up his beauty from the world,*
> *That when he please again to be himself,*
> *Being wanted, he may be more wondered at,*
> *By breaking through the foul and ugly mists*
> *Of vapours that did seem to strangle him...*
>
> *[I.ii]*

THE REAL PRINCE HAL

Historically, the battle of Shrewsbury took place when Henry IV had been on the throne for four years; it preceded his death by ten. In Shakespeare's version, the battle takes place little more than a year after the accession. The historic Henry was 36 at the time of the battle, but Shakespeare makes him seem much older.

Shakespeare's Hotspur is the same age as young Hal: their rivalry is central to the drama. In reality, Hotspur was a generation older than the prince. Although the legendary Hal was a young delinquent, a prodigal son, the historic Hal was a battle-hardened warrior. In 1399, at the age of 11, he took part in Richard II's campaign against the Irish, and was knighted for his services. Between 1401, when he was 13, and 1415, when he was 27, he led Henry

Here's "good Machiavel" indeed. Hal offers an assurance that he knows what he is doing, that he has a good aim in mind, and that he is not deceived by his low companions. On the other hand, this means that he is treating his low companions duplicitously; eventually he is bound, it seems, to betray them or let them down. Loyalty and disloyalty are thus interwoven. Furthermore, "foul and ugly mists" is a contemptuously reductive metaphor for the jovial company of Falstaff and his associates. Here the knowledge that Hal is manipulating others rather callously, as auxiliaries to his own eventual "reformation", is chilling. Hal is clearly intelligent and long-sighted; but who

IV's troops in resourceful campaigns against Owen Glendower's forces. Hotspur was initially his mentor.

Aged 13, Hal successfully headed the siege of Conway Castle. In March 1403, at 15, he was formally appointed the King's deputy in Wales. Prince Hal led a raiding party which burnt Glendower's home and took several captives, including a gentleman who offered generous and immediate ransom - to no avail: Hal ordered the death of all the captives. "Henry was a harsh commander, even in his youth," comments historian Margaret Wade Labarge.

By 1404, when he was 16, Hal commanded all efforts against the Welsh rebels, leading between 300 and 500 men-at-arms and 2,000 archers. In 1405, after a victory against a numerically superior Welsh force, the prince – pious as his Shakespearian counterpart at Agincourt – assured his father that "victory was not in a multitude of people, but in the power of God". Parliament formally congratulated Hal on his successful command in would wish him as a friend?

Shakespeare found that his company of actors included performers who were now so experienced and skilled that they could be entrusted to perform layered roles, in which the actor plays a character who is playing another character. One of the most richly variegated scenes, Act Two, Scene Four, moves to a climax as the comedy gives way increasingly to the serious. This is where Hal, playing the part of his father, has been heaping abuse on Falstaff – "a devil... in the likeness of an old fat man" – and Falstaff, playing Hal, has been making an increasingly fervent defence, his mask becoming transparent. The actor playing Falstaff playing Hal must let an anxious Falstaff show through:

Wales. Largely as a result of relentless pressure from the prince, Glendower's rebellion petered out. Hal then proceeded to numerous other duties: warden of the Cinque Ports, captain of Calais, leader of the King's council.

In short, the factual record of young Hal's martial and political career makes it difficult for us to credit those contemporaries who described him as "wild and reckless in his youth", or spoke of his devotion to Venus as well as Mars. Any recklessness or venereal joys would belong to the interstices in a very public life. As for the King's belief that Hal sought to overthrow his father: there were contemporaneous rumours to that effect, but it was said that the prince had persuaded the King of his loyalty.

In *Henry IV Part 1*, Hal

If to be old and merry be a sin, then many an old host that I know is damned. If to be fat be to be hated, then Pharaoh's lean kine are to be loved. No, my good Lord, banish Peto, banish Bardolph, banish Poins, but for sweet Jack Falstaff, kind Jack Falstaff, true Jack Falstaff, valiant Jack Falstaff – and therefore more valiant, being as he is old Jack Falstaff – banish not him thy Harry's company, banish not him thy Harry's company. Banish plump Jack, and banish all the world.

HAL: I do; I will.

[A knocking heard.]

[II.iv]

---

speaks tenderly to the slain Hotspur: "let my favours hide thy mangled face... / Thy ignomy sleep with thee in the grave, / But not remembered in thy epitaph" [V.iv]. In reality, Hotspur was not killed by Hal, though he was indeed slain at Shrewsbury. His corpse was then cut into pieces which were displayed in various locations in England – his head was impaled on one of the gates of York – after which the remains were sent to his widow for burial. She, originally Elizabeth Mortimer, who had married Hotspur when she was eight and he was 15, eventually married again: her second husband was Thomas, first Baron Camoys, who commanded the rearguard of the British army at Agincourt. Sometimes history's ironies surpass even Shakespeare's ∎

It's superbly managed. Falstaff wins laughter by citing the Bible in his defence – Genesis 41: Pharaoh's dream of lean kine [cattle] being interpreted by Joseph to portend years of famine – and by his bold hypocrisy: "valiant... valiant" from the man who ran away at Gads Hill; a "true" Falstaff who would abandon Peto, Bardolph and Poins. But he is indeed both old and merry: he has age-defying gusto. His tone, however, becomes increasingly earnest, modulating from the cajoling to the anxious and plaintive: it is almost that of a lover begging not to be rejected.

Nevertheless, when he says "Banish plump Jack, and banish all the world", his words recall the phrasing of the ceremony of baptism, in which the priest prays that the child will renounce the devil, the world, and the flesh. We are prepared, then, for Hal's emphatic "I do; I will". The acted King dissolves into the real prince, uttering an incisively clear warning of the eventual rejection – a warning given dramatically audible underlining by the "*knocking heard*". Here tragi-comic realism, thematic plenitude, moral subtlety and emotional drama are blended and variegated with virtuosity.

How do pseudo-digressions enrich this play?

A boldly experimental structural feature of *Henry IV Part I* is what might be called the "pseudo-digression". In his first soliloquy, Hal says that the time he spends among low companions is not really a digression from his progress to kingship; his apparent immersion in the tavern-world is part of that progress. In the play's very structure, Shakespeare is craftily surpassing Hal. He repeatedly offers material which at first may seem a digression from the progress of the drama but which is actually furthering the progress by enriching the moral discussion, the thematic orchestration, the kaleidoscope of comparisons, and the network of ironies. Hal has not really been wasting his time on trivia, and neither has Shakespeare.

Thus, the comic scenes are variously integrated with the main political matter. To take just one detail: in Act Two, Scene Four, Poins is puzzled by Hal's game with Francis, saying "What's the issue?", i.e. "What's the point?" But, for the astute Hal, the game is entirely germane to the political matter of being able to understand and manipulate others, and to the matter of preparation for the encounter with Hotspur. And it offers psychological relief, for Francis, summoned from two directions, enacts in comic key Hal's own situation, as he is interpellated – "summoned" – by both the court and the world of Falstaff. In *Henry IV Part 2*, Hal will underline this matter of "symbolic substitution" by taking the role of Francis himself, apparently delaying his accession to responsibility in the very act of mimicking Francis's "Anon, anon, sir!" – i.e. "At once: I'm coming now!"

A trickier instance may be the boldly sordid realism of Act Two, Scene One, in which we initially meet two grumbling carriers. They complain that the inn where they have been staying has declined greatly since Robin the ostler died – his death being precipitated by the rapid inflation in the cost of oats for horses. The current ostler has not prepared the horse for the journey; and the peas and beans supplied as horse fodder are so damp that they may give the horse "bots" (intestinal maggots). What's more, the landlord has denied the carriers a chamberpot, so that they have had to urinate in the fireplace; urine breeds fleas; both men are now covered in fleabites.

What makes this so realistic is precisely the convincing though unpredictable mundane detail, allied to our sense that this, like so many real events in our own lives, has no evident connection with the higher world of power politics and regal display. Precisely because it seems liberated from any plot-requirements, such material seems to hold the randomness of reality. Nevertheless, even here thematic connections lurk. The inn, which should be hospitable, is a treacherous location: the carriers are being treated meanly; Gadshill and the chamberlain are in league with thieves who may ambush these very travellers; the thieves believe they are protected by the presence of Hal.

The realism of the scene thus makes more clear, more telling, the nature of the low life with which Hal is associated. It makes more vivid the populace of the land which the noble power-seekers seek to divide to enrich themselves. It makes more acute the need for justice to be maintained in a world which lays many ambushes for the honest. And if it is hard to imagine that a change of ruler will result in an appropriate provision of chamberpots, even that ludicrous detail hints at a serious political implication: perhaps, until the carriers find their own political voice, their diverse legitimate needs will be ignored, regardless of whether a Richard or a Henry rules.

Those carriers represent honest, productive work. They are delivering turkeys, bacon and ginger to be traded at Charing Cross market. Compared with these humble suppliers of food, the lives of the quarrelling noblemen look strangely barren – even parasitic. Although Shakespeare was certainly no Marxist, we see why Marx was an enthusiastic Shakespearian.

TEN FACTS
ABOUT THE HISTORY PLAYS

1.

In 2012, to coincide with the Olympics, the BBC screened a version of the history plays under the title, *The Hollow Crown*. Richard was played by Ben Whishaw, Henry IV by Jeremy Irons, Henry V by Tom Hiddleston and Falstaff by Simon Russell Beale.

2.

It was in Richard II's reign that English, instead of French or Latin, emerged as the dominant language in England. Whereas John Gower hedged his bets by writing his *Confessio Amantis* (*c.*1390) in Latin, French and English, Chaucer wrote his masterpieces, notably *Troilus and Criseyde* and *The Canterbury Tales*, in English. When Bolingbroke claimed the throne in 1399 he did so in English, not French.

3.
Culture flourished under Richard II. In addition to the literary achievements of Chaucer, Gower and Froissart, the Wilton Diptych was painted and the famous tomb at Westminster Abbey created (ordered by Richard for himself and his first wife). Richard is also credited with being the first to use a pocket handkerchief.

4.
Henry IV was initially known as Henry Bolingbroke, as he was born at Bolingbroke Castle in Lincolnshire, a 13th-century hexagonal castle owned by John of Gaunt, his father.

5.
Sir Henry Percy, 1364-1403, is said to have been given his nickname 'Hotspur' by his Scottish foes in recognition of his alacrity in advancing and attacking.

6.
Hotspur was slain by an arrow from an unidentified archer and not, as Shakespeare has it, in combat with Hal.

7.
Hotspur is commemorated by the English Premier League football club, Tottenham Hotspur ('Spurs'), as he and his descendants sometimes resided at Tottenham.

8.

In the famous Laurence Olivier film of *Henry V*, the Battle of Agincourt was enacted at the Powerscourt Estate in Enniskerry, County Wicklow, in Ireland. Many English and French soldiers were played by Irish people, the production company paying a bounty to any man who brought his own horse.

9.

The cult movie *My Own Private Idaho* (1991, starring River Phoenix and Keanu Reeves) depicts two male hustlers, Mike and Scott, in Portland, Oregon. (Scott is the rebellious son of a high-ranking family.) They meet Bob Pigeon, a middle-aged gang-mentor. The film, inspired largely by the Hal-Falstaff relationship in Henry IV, credits Gus Van Sant and William Shakespeare as writers.

10.

John Danby, in *Shakespeare's Doctrine of Nature* (1949), argues that the playwright's study of Machiavelli is an important influence. Danby thinks that in the second tetralogy Shakespeare comes to terms with the "Machiavellianism" of the times as he saw them but believes that rebellion, even against a wrongful usurper, is never justifiable; from *Julius Caesar* onwards, he justifies tyrannicide, or regicide, but to do so moves away from English history to the camouflage of Roman, Danish, Scottish or Ancient British history.

What is it that makes Falstaff so extraordinary?

The character of Falstaff, while unique and phenomenal, had many sources. One was the ancient scapegoat – the symbolic bearer of the community's sins, who had to be punished and expelled from the community in order to strengthen it. Seen in this light, even the noble Oedipus and the plaintive Philoctetes, strange to say, stand among Falstaff's remote ancestors, each being at different times admired, reviled and appreciated.

The critic C.L.Barber has related Falstaff to the traditional figure of the Carnival King, the Lord of Misrule, who for a brief while is a centre of the anarchic festive celebration which is tolerated by authority and which, in the long run, strengthens authority. This view can be related to Mikhail Bakhtin's more radical theory of the carnivalesque, in which the vulgar, corporeal and subversive offer a valuable challenge to the rational, orderly and conservative. Arguably, however, the *Henry IV* plays proleptically expose the sentimentality in Bakhtin's theory by showing that though the carnivalesque may shrewdly criticise the conventional world, it remains parasitic on that world and may reinforce it.

Falstaff resembles a seedy cousin of that gigantic Green Knight – jolly but dangerous –

who, in the Gawain legend, mockingly disrupted the decorum of Arthur's court. Falstaff's other ancestors include: Silenus and Bacchus, the classical deities of celebration and alcoholic excess; Pyrgopolynices, the *miles gloriosus* or boastful warrior in a play of that title (*Miles Gloriosus*) by Plautus; and Friar Tuck, plump companion of the Robin Hood who stole from the rich to aid the poor. In the traditional Italian *commedia dell'arte*, the character called *Il Capitano* is a *miles gloriosus*; and the progeny of Pyrgopolynices also include Armado in *Love's Labour's Lost* and Ancient Pistol in *Henry IV Part 2*. But Armado and Pistol obviously lack the girth, intelligence, guile and charisma of Falstaff. (That surname "Falstaff", being homophonous with "false staff", suggests "treacherous supporter".)

Falstaff's popularity was soon established and has long endured. In 1640, Leonard Digges said that revivals of Jonson's *Volpone* and *The Alchemist* can barely break even, "yet let but Falstaff come, / Hal, Poins, the rest, you scarce shall have a room, / All is so pestered". Sir Thomas Palmer, in 1647, declares: "I could... tell how long / Falstaff from cracking nuts hath kept the throng." Later in the century, John Dryden termed Falstaff "the best of Comical Characters", explaining that he is "not properly one humour,

Opposite: A statue of Falstaff (1888) at the Gower Memorial, Bancroft Gardens, Stratford-upon-Avon.

but a Miscellany of Humours or Images, drawn from so many several men".

The 18th century prized wit, which again ensured Falstaff's prestige. In 1744 Corbyn Morris said that for "the sake of his *Wit*, you forgive his *Cowardice*; or rather, are fond of his *Cowardice* for the Occasions it gives to his *Wit*". Though Elizabeth Montagu found Falstaff "as ridiculous as witty, and as contemptible as entertaining", Dr Johnson decided that his wit made the "unimitable" Falstaff all the more dangerous a companion: "no man is more dangerous than he that with a will to corrupt, hath the power to please".

Later, the Romantic critic William Hazlitt revealed his radical sympathies when, comparing Falstaff with Hal, he declared: "Falstaff is the better man of the two." Even more enthusiastic was A.C.Bradley in his *Oxford Lectures on Poetry* (1909). He claimed that in creating Falstaff, Shakespeare "overshot the mark". Bradley explains: "He created so extraordinary a being, and fixed him so firmly on the intellectual throne, that when he sought to dethrone him he could not." Bradley deemed the rejection of Falstaff by Hal in *Henry IV Part 2* a critically crucial scene, and many subsequent critical discussions hinged on this part of the drama.

The rejection, most commentators agree, was morally and politically necessary. It is the manner and tone of the rejection which have proved controversial. Was Hal needlessly harsh? Does John of Lancaster's approval of Hal's conduct really endorse it? Or is John's commendation Shakespeare's condemnation? The last two questions are usually answered with, respectively, a no and a yes. John's treacherous conduct at Gaultree Forest being fresh in our mind, his approval is a virtual condemnation. As for the harshness of Hal's response, it underlines the point made repeatedly in these histories: political success requires a degree of ruthlessness. Derek Traversi made this notion the main theme of his study, *Shakespeare from 'Richard II' to 'Henry V'*. Traversi says of Hal:

> The loss in human qualities which appears, in these plays, to be involved in the very fact of political success gives a tragic undertone to his triumphant progress.

Gradually,

> the function of Falstaff enters into its full subtlety, combining the vicious role of the fat knight as misleader of youth and incarnation of anarchy with that of vivid human commentator on the detached inhumanity which political ability, once the natural bonds of an orderly society have been broken, seems increasingly to imply.

Shakespeare's Falstaff is uniquely talented. He is the poet laureate of larceny, the disgraceful doyen of decadence, the inspiring patron of the dissipated. Though breathlessly obese, he is a lithe gymnast in sophistical logic; while hedonistically anti-intellectual, he is a fluent thesaurus of learned allusions. His vocabulary spans the vulgar, the lyrical, the biblical and the fantastic. In his first scene, with orotund and alliterative fluency, he flatteringly portrays nocturnal thieves as "Diana's foresters, gentlemen of the shade, minions of the moon" [I.ii]. An astute commentator, Tony Nuttall, has remarked (in *A New Mimesis*):

> Falstaff speaks a golden Shakespearean English which makes him the centre of a small world of joy wherever he goes. Above all, in the very jaws of senility and death, he is life, and whenever he comes near there is a real danger that the great warlords will be seen for what they perhaps are – mere bloody men, agents of death.

Even this perceptive view simplifies the complexities of Falstaff, who is, for his wretched conscripts, not life but death – "I have led my ragamuffins where they are peppered" (*Part 1*, V.iii) – and, repeatedly, he is an agent of egoistic exploitation. He breaks promises, cheats and is treacherous. In *Part 2* he cheats the hostess by failing to pay bills; he promises to marry her while bedding Doll Tearsheet; and he cheats Shallow out of the colossal sum (then) of a thousand pounds. When he is recruiting troops in *Part 1*, he lets the able-bodied bribe their way to freedom, while retaining the ragged and forlorn. Hal remarks of the conscripts: "I did never see such pitiful rascals" (IV.ii). Yet even here, Falstaff, ever resourceful in excusing his own vices, produces a telling defence. He says:

> *Tut, tut, good enough to toss; food for powder,*
> *food for powder; they'll fill a pit as well as better.*
> *Tush, man, mortal men, mortal men.*

In other words, if a battle requires cannon-fodder, isn't it better that those who perish should be the wretched and feeble, rather than the upstanding and able? Falstaff reminds us that repeatedly, in real-life modern warfare, it is the recruits who are fit enough to pass the medical examination who become eligible to meet death in battle, while, with anti-Darwinian logic, the unfit, disqualified from military service, are saved for posterity and procreation.

Falstaff is the resourceful hierophant of hypocrisy, complaining to Hal, "Thou... art indeed able to corrupt a saint" (I.ii), and quoting the Bible liberally to justify his wayward course. He veers between arrogance and self-pity, between bullying and sentimentality. As an actor, he is a protean virtuoso; and Hal, who is deliberately developing skills as a mimic and actor as a means to power, is fascinated by the veteran's talents. Hal delights in Falstaff's company, but is never fooled by him; there is always a critical distance.

The obese Falstaff is the visible incarnation of appetite. In Shakespeare's imagination, "appetite" was a key term connoting voracity of various kinds: alimentary greed, illicit sexual desire and anarchic ambition. (In *Troilus and Cressida*, Ulysses declares that appetite is "an universal wolf".) To Alan Sinfield, however, Falstaff, "with his drinking, eating, jesting, and fatness... embodies unmasculine *relaxation*... The masculine, conversely, is represented as taut, often with phallic connotation" (*Faultlines*, 1992). Yet when we see Falstaff converting matters of religion, morality, learning, warfare and politics into the stuff of fun and games, sheer mirth proves potently subversive. Just as he overcomes the hostess's resistance, Falstaff seduces numerous critics. Listen, for instance, to Ronald Knowles:

As art intervening in history, comedy subverting chronicle, Falstaff ultimately both suggests and burlesques an ideal order of value which appraises the dramatised historical actuality of the feudal world... The Epilogue [of *Henry IV Part 2*] plays with the idea of the audience as creditor owed a successful play. On the contrary,

Orson Welles (Falstaff) and Jeanne Moreau (Doll Tearsheet) in Chimes at Midnight
(1966), which, according to the New York Times, *"may be the greatest
Shakespearean film ever made, bar none". Welles himself considered it to be his best
film, stating in a 1982 BBC interview: "I succeeded more completely with that
[*Chimes at Midnight*], in my view, than with anything else."*

by the end of *Henry IV Parts I and II* Shakespeare
knows that we are in Falstaff's debt, and we owe
him our love.

A more astringent conclusion is offered by
Herschel Baker:

If Falstaff, incapable of intellectual torpor and
indifferent to the curbs that shackle most of us,
represents the lawless ease and freedom that

every man desires and most men never find, he also represents destruction.

Shakespeare's Falstaff is more than a character. He is a phenomenon. Like Hamlet and Don Quixote, he is: (i) immediately and distinctively recognisable; (ii) of enduring cultural significance; (iii) easily capable of exceeding his designated literary role.

Turgenev once said that Hamlet and Don Quixote represent the two ends of the axle-tree on which human nature turns, Hamlet representing rationality which inhibits action, Don Quixote being able to act but in ways which are irrational. Falstaff and Hal could be said to represent a similarly enduring opposition in human nature. Falstaff represents the appeal of the anarchically and egoistically hedonistic: sheer selfish pleasure. Hal represents a will to power which requires the rational control or expulsion of the anarchic: calculated conquest. It's tempting to say that in Freudian terms Falstaff is the rebellious id, and Hal's father the stern superego; but the temptation should probably be avoided, for this father is patently fallible, and Freud's id, for all its potency, is faceless and heartless: it lacks the twinkling-eyed winning roguishness of Falstaff at his best.

HENRY IV
PART 2

A summary of the plot

Act One

The Induction, by "Rumour", says that the "crafty-sick" Northumberland will receive false news that his son Hotspur has slain Hal at the Battle of Shrewsbury. In the play's opening scene, Northumberland first hears that, but soon hears the truth: that Hotspur was slain by Hal. Northumberland says: "These news, / Having been well, that would have made me sick, / Being sick, have in some measure made me well". But he then pronounces a deranged curse:

> Let heaven kiss earth! Now let not Nature's
> hand
> Keep the wild flood confined! Let order die!...
> But let one spirit of the first-born Cain
> Reign in all bosoms, that, each heart being set
> On bloody courses, the rude scene may end,
> And darkness be the burier of the dead!

Morton and Lord Bardolph tell him that the rebels have been strengthened by the Archbishop of York, who "Turns insurrection to religion": he gives religious warrant to the cause, invoking "the blood / Of fair King Richard, scraped from Pomfret stones". The once-feckless King has become a martyr yielding holy relics.

In London, Falstaff, complaining of the gout or

the pox – or both – is rebuked by the Lord Chief Justice. Falstaff says he is afflicted by deafness, and remarks that the King is said to be suffering from apoplexy. (Diseases of various kinds seem widespread.) The conspirators, the Archbishop of York, Mowbray, Lord Bardolph and Hastings, consider their chances of success, noting that the fickle populace have turned against Henry IV and now favour Richard's memory.

Act Two

Meanwhile, the hostess seeks to have Falstaff arrested for debt and for breach of promise to marry, but he wins her over. Hal tells Poins that though he regrets inwardly the King's illness, to display his grief would be regarded as hypocrisy. Lady Percy, widow of Hotspur, urges Northumberland not to support the rebels. At a tavern, there is a brawl involving Falstaff, Bardolph and boastful Pistol; Bardolph drives Pistol away. Falstaff laments to Doll: "I am old, I am old." Hal and Poins eavesdrop on Falstaff, hearing the slanders from which the fat knight later tries to exculpate himself.

Act Three

At court, King Henry laments that he has sleepless nights – "Uneasy lies the head that wears a crown" – and he notes that Richard II had prophesied truly that Northumberland would one day rebel against Henry. Warwick tells Henry that Glendower is dead.

In Gloucestershire, Falstaff meets old Shallow and Silence. Falstaff seeks recruits, but is quite willing to let some of them bribe their way out of service.

Act Four

At Gaultree forest, the rebel leaders meet the leaders of the King's forces. Prince John assures the rebels that their grievances will be redressed, saying that peace should prevail. The rebels are persuaded to dismiss their troops. Prince John, however, has not dismissed his own forces, and treacherously arrests the rebel leaders as traitors; he sentences them to death.

The King hears the news of the rebels' defeat, but – echoing Northumberland in Act One, Scene One – finds that "these good news make me sick", exacerbating his illness. Prince Hal, watching at the King's bedside, thinks that the King has died, and accordingly carries off the crown. Henry IV wakes and is angered by Hal's action, but Hal persuades the King of his deep loyalty.

Act Five

After the King's death, Hal, now Henry V, reassures the Lord Chief Justice of his support. The hostess and Doll Tearsheet are arrested by beadles. Falstaff has hastened to London, thinking that Hal will make him the Lord Chief Justice, but is curtly dismissed. Prince John praises Hal's "fair proceeding" [V.v] and prophesies that Henry V will lead an army against France.

What is *Henry IV Part 2* about?

Although the historical events follow directly from those in *Part 1*, a pall of ageing, disease and decrepitude seems to have fallen on numerous characters. The very Induction is uttered by Rumour – who depicts himself as the anarchically unhealthy or illegitimate brother of Truth. Whereas *Part 1* centred on the developing contest between two young contenders for the throne, Hal and Hotspur, *Part 2* shows pervasively the process of ageing and decay. Richard II, addressing Northumberland, had warned the usurpers:

> *Yet know, my master, God omnipotent,*
> *Is mustering in the clouds, on our behalf,*
> *Armies of pestilence; and they shall strike*
> *Your children yet unborn and unbegot..*
>
> *[III.iii]*

Northumberland, Falstaff, Henry IV, Shallow, Silence: all become personally aware of disease, decline and the remorseless passage of time. "We are time's subjects," says Hastings in Act One. John Gower, the medieval poet, declared: "The King and his people are like the head and the body: where the head is infirm, the body is infirm." Shakespeare's play reflects this.* What has happened is that the "body politic" is diseased, as a consequence of Bolingbroke's act of usurpation; and this is indicated in the play by a multiple synecdoche: different elements indicate the great central problem. Even Falstaff's almost-empty purse is, he says, suffering from disease: "this consumption of the purse; borrowing only lingers and lingers it out, but the disease is incurable" [I.ii]. Once again, the stature of Richard II seems to increase posthumously as his prophecy of "pestilence" appears to be fulfilled.

In Gloucestershire, Falstaff meets not only his former associates, the ageing Shallow and Silence (with the servant Davy), but also some recruits whose very names – in four out of five cases – echo that thematic sense of decrepitude: Mouldy, Wart, Shadow and Feeble; the fifth recruit, Bullcalf, is unwell. The increase in the attention given to "low" characters shows that Shakespeare is increasingly concerned to extend the discussion of statecraft and the political by offering an apparently contrasting and challenging context.

*Ironically, Henry IV had said: "If any plague hang over us, 'tis he" – referring to the misunderstood Hal.

94

*Klaus Glowalla as King Henry IV and Thomas Thieme as Henry Prince of Wales,
in* Henry IV *at Theater Magdeburg (1977)*

Hal seems world-weary when we initially meet him in Act Two, Scene Two: his first words are "Before God, I am exceeding weary". There is also evidence of moral decline: Northumberland invokes chaos, and later betrays his fellow-rebels; Falstaff is now markedly less the jolly giant than the ruthless con-man; and the rebels are defeated by a Machiavellian trick by Prince John. At least Hal, on becoming King Henry V, brings new vigour and decisiveness to the throne; but his dismissal, in chilly tones, of Falstaff and the fat knight's associates (along with the arrest of the hostess and Doll) may suggest that Hal now errs on the side of harshness.

Andrew Dickson says of Hal:

His education as a prince, one of the major
strands in the *Henry IV* plays, has been achieved,
but Shakespeare does not hide from us its
personal cost, nor does he cosset us by insisting
that the perfect prince has to be a perfect man.

The scene in which the hostess and Doll are
carried off by beadles (with the sinister names
"Fang" and "Snare") anticipates the scene in
Measure for Measure in which the harsh rule of
the hypocritical Angelo is inaugurated by a purge
of Vienna's brothels. In the event, Angelo proves
(unlike Hal) to be wicked, but both cases suggest
that authority has acted with an excess of
puritanical zeal.

R.A.Law argued in 1927 that *Part 2* differed
from *Part 1* in owing a strong debt to the Morality
play tradition: here Hal must choose Justice and
eschew Misrule; the various stylised names recall
the conventions of Moralities. Law also points out
some of the subtle linkages between scenes. In Act
Three, Scene One, Henry IV reminiscences about
the reign of Richard II; in the following scene,
Shallow, in a different key, reminisces about
Richard's era, recalling Mowbray and John of
Gaunt. Again, in Act Five, Scene One, Davy asks
Justice Shallow to "countenance" Visor, a rogue
who happens to be a friend of Davy's; but Shallow

firmly declines to do so. (The name "Visor" indicates that he wears a mask to rob.) In the following scene, the Lord Chief Justice recalls the time when he refused to be lenient to a rogue who happened to be a crony of Hal's. Both Justice Shallow in Gloucestershire and the Lord Chief Justice in London are admirably incorruptible. (In *Henry IV Part I*, we recall, Hal had saved Falstaff from arrest by the Sheriff.) By such means, Shakespeare, while providing contrast and diversity, yet offers shrewd co-ordination.

Another example is the theme of insomnia. In Act Three, Scene One, the King laments that, racked by cares, he is denied sleep, though he enjoys regal luxuries, whereas lowly people and even a wind-tossed ship-boy enjoy restful slumbers. In the next scene, Falstaff agrees with Shallow that they have both "heard the chimes at midnight" in their youthful pursuit of women: they "lay all night in the Windmill' – probably a brothel – and knew the bona-roba or courtesan, the aptly-named Jane Nightwork. The insomnia of anxiety and guilt is thus contrasted with the insomnia of the youthful hedonists. In *Henry V*, Act Four, Scene One, Hal will reflect bitterly that a "wretched slave" enjoys ample sleep, whereas the King, recompensed only by "ceremony", must suffer wakeful nights, to "maintain the peace" of the lowly. (The reference to peace is incongruous, given that Hal is here wakeful because he is moving among the troops on the eve of the great battle.)

What is the mood of *Henry IV Part 2*?

Henry IV Part 2 is sometimes termed Shakespeare's first tragi-comedy. It is a highly sophisticated drama in which high and low scenes are co-ordinated by related themes – ageing, ailing, moral and physical disease and decrepitude – which precipitate numerous symptomatic details, from Falstaff's pox or gout and "consumption of the purse" to the King's "apoplexy" and Bullcalf's "whoreson cold". Rebellions are "rank diseases". It's an ailing kingdom, which perhaps needs new blood – young Hal in command – or bloodletting: the warfare in France foretold by Prince John and the Epilogue.

Anton Chekhov (1860-1904) became famed for plays which had a distinctive tragi-comic quality: an atmospheric 'mood-music' in which laughter is close to tears, in which nostalgic melancholy infiltrates the jocular and absurd. We encounter characters who are ludicrous, comical and pathetic, ineffectual yet touching in their vulnerability. In *Uncle Vanya*, *Three Sisters* and *The Cherry Orchard*, characters often talk across each other rather than with each other, and nostalgia's melancholy pervades the discussions like a dank mist dampening enthusiasms and hopes.

Such effects have an obvious source in Shakespeare's *Henry IV Part 2*, and, in particular, in those Gloucestershire scenes featuring Falstaff, Shallow and Silence. The dialogue roams from present to past and back, recalling wild times of long ago, when Shallow was "lusty Shallow" (commanding the "bona-robas", the courtesans), and Falstaff was page boy to Mowbray; but it notes repeatedly the tally of mortality: "And to see how many of my old acquaintance are dead!" [III.ii]. Silence comments: "We shall all follow, cousin"; and Shallow rejoins:

> *Certain, 'tis certain, very sure, very sure. Death (as the Psalmist saith) is certain to all: all shall die. How a good yoke of bullocks at Stamford fair?'*
> [III.ii]

Comic and sad reminiscences, cited and enacted reminders of ageing and mortality, and the perennial work of the countryside: all are interwoven. The scene generates an atmosphere which is partly melancholy and autumnal, partly practical (Shallow gives clear directions to Davy about such work as sowing) and partly satiric: Falstaff – here a pot calling the kettle black – says that Shallow is a boastful liar, though he was "lecherous as a monkey".

As in Chekhov, the comedy has a melancholy music. In Act Two of *The Cherry Orchard*, the music of melancholy dialogue is accompanied by a song to a guitar; and in *Henry IV Part 2*, Act Five, Scene Three, when Shallow and Silence are becoming drunkenly incoherent, Silence's songs of youthful merriment provide an ironic refrain. Shakespeare, of course, integrates the Gloucestershire scenes amply with the main action, not only by their thematic connections, but also by the plot-matter. Falstaff is visiting Gloucestershire in course of a corrupt recruiting campaign, ostensibly to muster soldiers to fight for the King; and later Pistol will arrive breathlessly to tell Falstaff of the King's death, so that Falstaff thinks he will soon command all the justices of the land – including Justice Shallow, from whom he "borrows" a thousand pounds.

Expressionist art, characterised by the paintings of Edvard Munch and Vincent Van Gogh, is art defined by distortions of perspective, or strange departures from straightforward realism, which generate a peculiar vision, usually intense, sometimes nightmarish. In the atmospheric orchestration of *Henry IV Part 2*, where every region of the realm seems to be infiltrated by reminders of mortality, Shakespeare is anticipating Expressionism. In this play he manipulates time – variously accelerating it, retarding it, and accentuating its pressure – and inflects realism towards the Expressionist art of the future. The characterisations are strong and vivid, and the comedy at the tavern is often rumbustious, but all contribute to the controlling vision dominated by time, entropy, decay, disease, decline. What makes that vision so fully political is that it apparently extends beyond the political: striving people, motivated by greed, fear, ambition, pleasure, power, are all mocked by time and mortality.

HENRY V

A summary of the plot

Act One
The wily Archbishop of Canterbury assures Henry V that the King's claim to the throne of France is valid. A French ambassador bears a scornful message and a gift of tennis balls to Henry from the Dauphin ("Dolphin"). Henry says that war will now follow.

Act Two
At Southampton, the King arrests and sentences to death Scroop, Cambridge and Grey, who have conspired against him. In London, Falstaff is mortally ill, and dies. Mistress Quickly, the hostess, discusses the death with Bardolph, Nym, Pistol and the boy.

Act Three
In France, at the siege of Harfleur ("Harflew"), Henry rallies his troops, whose nationalities include Welsh, Scottish and Irish. After a threatening speech from Henry, the Governor opens the city's gates to the British. Later, the battle of Agincourt impends. The French are confident of victory, and Henry concedes that his troops are weakened by sickness.

Act Four
In disguise, Henry moves among his forces, and is

challenged by two soldiers, Bates and Williams: Williams argues that the King is responsible for the fate of the souls of his men who die in battle. Later, privately, Henry prays for God's aid, the British being greatly outnumbered, and then, with stirring rhetoric, urges his men to action. The great battle ensues, and results in an astonishing victory for the British. Henry is told that there are 10,000 French dead but only 29 British. God must be credited, says the King.

Act Five

In the aftermath of the victory, Henry woos and wins Katherine, the French princess. It seems that an era of peace between England and France has at last been established. The Epilogue, however, warns of woe to come.

Why is *Henry V* now seen as a paradoxical play?

Henry V is a classic example of the janiform text: one which, like the god Janus, seems to face in opposite directions at the same time, being radically paradoxical. It long had the reputation of being a straightforward patriotic play, a celebration of the glamorous and heroic Henry V; but in recent years, widespread scepticism regarding warfare, patriotism and martial rhetoric has been reflected in critical attention to the play's contrapuntal features. "Is it a celebration of national glory, with Henry a truly heroic warrior prince?" asks Richard Dutton. "Or is it a dark satire on warfare and the abuses of power...?"

Among those who gave voice to the patriotic (and romantic) view was Thomas Carlyle in 1841:

> That battle of Agincourt strikes me as one of the most perfect things, in its sort, we anywhere have of Shakespeare's. The description of the two hosts: the worn-out, jaded English; the dread hour, big with destiny, when the battle shall begin; and then that deathless valour: "Ye good yeomen, whose limbs were made in England!" There is a noble Patriotism in it, – far other than the "indifference" you sometimes hear ascribed to Shakespeare. A true English heart breathes, calm and strong, through the whole business; not boisterous, protrusive; all the better for that. There is a sound in it like the ring of steel. This man too had a right stroke in him, had it come to that!

Sidney Lee, in 1908, wrote that alone in Shakespeare's gallery of monarchs, Henry was portrayed as evoking "a joyous sense of satisfaction in the high potentialities of human character and a sense of pride among Englishmen". In 1964, A.C. Sprague found the play, though "by no means without shadows... a clear, straightforward history", while Michael Quinn, five years later, saw Hal as "an ordinary man called to an extraordinary office and fulfilling it magnificently".

Among those who didn't warm to Shakespeare's portrait of Henry V were, not surprisingly, two illustrious Irishmen. W.B. Yeats, in *Ideas of Good and Evil* (1903), found Henry "as remorseless and undistinguished as some natural force", while the ever-lucid George Bernard Shaw, in *Dramatic Opinions and Essays* (1907), wrote:

> One can hardly forgive Shakespeare quite for the worldly phase in which he tried to thrust such a Jingo hero as his Harry V down our throats. The combination of conventional propriety and brute masterfulness in his public capacity with a low-lived blackguardism in his private tastes is not a pleasant one... His popularity, therefore, is like that of a prizefighter: nobody feels for him as for Romeo or Hamlet.

By the 1980s, both Henry, and Shakespeare's portrayal of him, were often viewed sceptically. Nevertheless, Stephen Greenblatt, a conservative 'New Historicist', argued in 1985 that though the play "continually awakens" subversive doubts, they serve paradoxically to intensify the power of the king and his war, even while they cast shadows upon this power... The very doubts that Shakespeare raises serve not to rob the king of his charisma but to heighten it, precisely as they heighten the theatrical interest of the play...

In *Political Shakespeare*, 1985, Jonathan Dollimore and Alan Sinfield, who termed themselves 'cultural materialists' (i.e. neo-Marxists), found *Henry V* replete with ideological tensions and contradictions:

Even in this play, which is often assumed to be the one where Shakespeare is closest to state propaganda, the construction of ideology is complex – even as it consolidates, it betrays inherent instability... Systematically, antagonism is reworked as subordination or supportive alignment...

For instance, the traitors arrested by the King at Southampton express not only penitence but gratitude that they have been caught by him: foes become supporters. The dramatised conquest of France, claim Dollimore and Sinfield, was "a displaced, imaginary solution" of the intractable problem of subjugating Ireland. We may recall (a) the presence of the Irish Macmorris among Henry's supporters, and (b) the Chorus which, at

Laurence Olivier won a special Academy Award for his outstanding achievement as actor, producer and director in the 1944 film Henry V.

the start of Act Five, wishes Essex a victorious campaign against the Irish rebels. Furthermore, when Henry is wooing Katherine, he says that her acquiescence will mean that – among other acquisitions – "Ireland is thine". Shakespeare, however, complicates matters by letting Macmorris voice resentment. When Fluellen mentions his "nation", Macmorris furiously responds:

> *Of my nation? What ish my nation? Ish a villain, and a bastard, and a knave, and a rascal? What ish my nation? Who talks of my nation?*
>
> *[II.ii]*

Here Macmorris voices the indignation of a man who knows that the Irish have long been treated with scorn by English propagandists. In Shakespeare's day, after Macmorris's fictional time, that scorn would be expressed, notoriously, by Edmund Spenser, who, in *A View of the Present State of Ireland* (1596), termed the Irish "that salvage [savage] nation", the people "stubborn", the leaders "barbarous and bastard-like".

How seriously should we take the romantic view?

Part of *Henry V* is undoubtedly patriotic, glorifying Henry and his achievements. There are numerous celebrated passages of stirring oratory, the kind that makes one feel proud to be British; rhetoric to rally the nation in times of war and crisis. This is the side emphasised in Laurence Olivier's famous film of 1944, dedicated to our paratroops and airborne commandos.

I saw that film when it was first released, at a time when, after D-Day, the Allied armies were battling their way through France towards the Rhine. The cinema was packed; the audience clamorously cheered the British victory at Agincourt, and heartily applauded the screen at the end, before standing to attention – as was then customary – for the National Anthem.

The Olivier film was characterised by directorial panache: there were bold juxtapositions of the stylised and the realistic, of the Elizabethan and the modern. If the French (particularly the Dauphin) were sometimes risibly mocked, this seemed fair play, given that recently the Vichy French had been fighting for Hitler. The film offered "Shakespeare for the people": Shakespeare made vividly accessible and enjoyable even for schoolchildren. The very use of colour was a defiant gesture, since wartime economy measures had meant that British films were customarily monochrome.

Of course, Olivier deleted most of the subversive subtext: for instance, the conspirators' scene was omitted, and so was Henry's order to kill the French prisoners. Shakespeare would not have been surprised: as a practical man of the playhouse (actor, scriptwriter, shareholder, and director – inevitably, though the title 'director' was not then used), he knew that a Shakespearian script was a body of material to be cut, augmented and variously adapted according to changing circumstances.

If you seek patriotic rhetoric, Shakespeare's *Henry V* is a treasure-house of it. The most famous example is the "band of brothers" speech. Henry argues that though the British are outnumbered, "The fewer men, the greater share of honour".

Anyone who lacks the stomach for the fight is welcome to depart; but the survivors will proudly recall their share in the victory:

> *This story shall the good man teach his son;*
> *And Crispin Crispian shall ne'er go by,*
> *From this day to the ending of the world,*
> *But we in it shall be rememberèd;*
> *We few, we happy few, we band of brothers:*
> *For he today that sheds his blood with me*
> *Shall be my brother: be he ne'er so vile,*
> *This day shall gentle his condition;*
> *And gentlemen in England, now a-bed,*
> *Shall think themselves accursed they were not*
> *here,*
> *And hold their manhoods cheap whiles any speaks*
> *That fought with us upon Saint Crispin's day.*
> *[IV.iii]*

The critic David Margolies says that this speech "oozes honour, military glory, love of country and self-sacrifice", and claims that it forms one of the first instances in English Literature of solidarity and comradeship being linked to success in battle. Henry shrewdly links the fighters to the twin brothers, Saints Crispin and Crispinian, who, according to one of their diverse legends, lived in the third century A.D., worked as cobblers, and were martyred in 297 at Soissons in France for preaching Christianity. Another legend held that they became cobblers at Faversham in Kent. Either way, the invocation of these two saints not only glamorises the date, the saints' day, October 25th; it also lends a veneer of sanctity to the bloody action which will ensue.

Furthermore, in May 1414, French Armagnac forces, opposed to French Burgundians, had sacked Soissons, massacring the male citizens, raping the women – even the nuns – and despoiling the churches. The leader of those merciless marauders was Jean, Duke of Bourbon, who in 1415 became a leader of troops at Agincourt. Juliet Barker suggests that the two cobbler-martyrs of Soissons were then avenged, for the Duke of Bourbon was captured at Agincourt and died in captivity in England. The historic Henry inaugurated Masses in honour of Crispin and Crispinian.

In the play, Henry's democratic appeal to the "band of brothers" is highly attractive but largely specious: Williams, after the battle, is treated by Henry not as his brother but merely as "this fellow". Nevertheless, the versions of that "band of brothers" speech in both the Olivier and the Branagh films give durable evidence of the power of such martial rhetoric.

The play's patriotic bias is evident in the depiction of the French. The Dauphin is depicted as an arrogant and naive boaster, whereas the French King and the Constable both pay warm tribute to Hal and his heritage, as when they praise the prowess of the Black Prince. The Constable mocks the Dauphin's vaunted prowess.

Dr Johnson said: "Patriotism is the last refuge of a scoundrel" – and sometimes it may be. At other times, the patriotic spirit in Britain has been vindicated, as when, in the Great War, the British fought the forces of Kaiser Wilhelm II, who had long meditated a war of imperialistic aggression, and as when, in World War Two, the British fought the forces of Adolf Hitler, whose early martial successes were applauded by that same rabidly anti-Semitic Kaiser Wilhelm.

King Richard's downfall led eventually to the emergence of Henry V, probably the most charismatically successful British monarch known to the Elizabethans. That charisma is splendidly rendered and magnified by Shakespeare's eloquence. Observed through half-shut eyes, the four plays which reach a climax in *Henry V* can look like a nationalistic epic entitled "The Evolution of the Ideal Monarch". Shakespeare's eyes, however, are wide open. He shows us the shrewd Machiavellianism – albeit here good (i.e. patriotic) Machiavellianism – which in Shakespeare's work is usually a characteristic of the successful political leader.

Interweaving the patriotic material of the play, however, we find a substantial quantity of subversive material which casts a fiercely critical light on Henry V, his achievements and even on patriotic warfare generally. That is the other face of Janus.

CENSORING *HENRY V*

Annabel Patterson has argued strongly that *Henry V* was vigorously censored. Editors believe that the long 1623 version was printed from Shakespeare's manuscript of the play. The implication is that the short version staged during his lifetime is short because of cuts and not because Shakespeare had not yet written some parts.

The short version of *Henry V* lacks all the Choruses, including the Chorus in which Essex is praised. Furthermore, it lacks Act One, Scene One, which shows rather Machiavellian churchmen conspiring to support the war in France in order to protect the church's wealth. It lacks the passage in which the King is blamed for breaking Falstaff's heart. It lacks, too, most of the bloodcurdling speech made by Henry at the gates of Harfleur, the speech in which he threatens to let his troops rape the women and massacre infants.

The gentle mockery of the Scottish captain Jamy in Act Three, Scene Two, is also cut (perhaps because the Scottish-born James VI would have disliked it). And while some of these excisions may have been made merely to shorten the play for performance, it is notable that the excisions remove not only the dangerous reference to Essex but also much of that subversive subtext which makes us look with some suspicion on Henry's conduct ∎

THE "MIRACLE" OF AGINCOURT

In the play, the British victory, against immense odds, is so overwhelming that, in Henry's view, it is miraculous. A "fresh" French army with 60,000 fighting men (according to Westmorland and Exeter) is trounced by a weary British army with only 12,000. What was the truth?

On the eve of battle, the British troops were weakened by hunger, long marches and illness (mainly dysentery), and were indeed outnumbered by the eager, well-fed and heavily armoured French. Historians disagree about the numerical disparity. One revisionist view contends that the French army numbered 12,000 to the British 9,000, a ratio of 4:3, but this seems to minimise French numbers and maximise British ones. More plausibly, Juliet Barker, in her *Agincourt* (2005), says that the British were outnumbered "at least four to one and possibly as much as six to one". She suggests figures of about 6,000 for the British and 36,000 for the French.

Given the discrepancies, we may be inclined to

trust a man who was actually there. Jehan de Wavrin, who saw the action from the French lines, and whose estimate is in line with Juliet Barker's, asserts that "the French were in number fully six times as many as the English". Wavrin's father and older brother were slain in the battle fighting for France, so it is unlikely he would flatter the English when he specified the disparity.

As for the casualties, estimates again vary hugely. Some English sources have estimated between 1,500 and 11,000 French died, with the English dead perhaps as few as 100. What is certain is that the earliest chroniclers who were eyewitnesses – two French and one British – emphasised that although the British had been grossly outnumbered by the French, the French losses far exceeded the British. Accordingly, many later British readers will have deemed as plausible as any the figures given by the historian A.R. Myers, setting the French losses at about 7,000, the British at about 500: still an astonishing result.

Standard explanations of the British victory are:

1. The British, though weary, were well-trained, and used a very effective combination of longbow archers and men-at-arms, the archers being protected by pointed stakes.

2. The French, though fresh and well supplied, were badly led and disorderly, their units ill-coordinated.

3. The wet weather helped the British: the heavily

armoured French cavalry became bogged down in muddy ploughed land; fallen combatants struggled in the mire.

4. The British longbow had a far greater range and more rapid rate of discharge than the French bolt-firing crossbow.

5. A contemporaneous account by a monk of St Denis also says that wounded and panicking horses galloped back through the French infantry, scattering and trampling them. The crowded French troops impeded each other, falling confusedly into the quagmire.

After the British longbow-arrows had brought down many men and horses, the lightly armoured and therefore relatively nimble British bowmen could join their men-at-arms in stabbing, hacking and bludgeoning their fallen, struggling adversaries.

According to English and French accounts, Henry took part in the hand-to-hand fighting, and received an axe-blow to the head which knocked off a piece of the crown that was part of his helmet. In the play, as in reality, Henry is too piously modest to have his "bruised helmet" displayed on his return. In any case, the play, by not specifying various material circumstances listed above (the muddy ground, the firing-rate of the longbow, etc,), emphasises the apparent dependence of the victory on divine favour.

How subversive is the play's subtext?

Henry's motivation and ambition are questioned from the beginning. The churchmen in the opening scene make clear that to protect the church's wealth from parliamentary demands, they will support Henry's claim to France, for he will then favour the church. This obviously calls in question the justification for war that the Archbishop will provide. In Kenneth Branagh's film, this opening scene had a sinister, conspiratorial atmosphere.

When the Archbishop provides his justification for the King's claim to France, it is a longwinded rigmarole, tedious rather than convincing. (In Laurence Olivier's film, it was played as farcical comedy; in Branagh's, the Archbishop's line "So that, as clear as is the summer sun" prompted sarcastic laughter from the noblemen.) Indeed, this versification of Holinshed was surely meant to seem a comic rigmarole, given its mind-numbing catalogue of locations, names, dates, fussy details and irritating repetitions. John Fletcher confirms this view in his play *The Noble Gentleman* (*c.* 1624-26), which contains a direct parody of the Archbishop's arguments. In *The Noble Gentleman*, the speaker is a madman, Shatillion, who advances a crazy claim to the French throne, amplifying the prolixity and needless naming which are tell-tale signs in the original. Arguably, the rightful English claimant to the French throne was not Henry V but Edmund Mortimer. We may, in any case, recall the Machiavellian advice given by the dying Henry IV to his son: "busy giddy minds / With foreign quarrels" [IV.v]. Then, as now, the distraction of a foreign war was a useful way of keeping a troublesome populace in line.

The play is constantly pointing to the realities behind the rhetoric. In Act Two, for instance, we are told of the poignant death of Falstaff, abandoned by Henry, his former friend, when he ascended the throne. Shortly before the news, the hostess says: "The King has killed his heart." While the Chorus of Act Two assures us that "the youth of England" are enthusiastic for war, and "honour's thought / Reigns solely in the breast of every man", the following scene shows a sordid quarrel between Nym and Pistol.

Similarly, in Act Three, at the siege of Harfleur, Henry makes his stirring speech beginning "Once more unto the breach, dear friends" – but his rhetoric has little effect on Nym, Bardolph and Pistol. The "boy" tells us that they are cowardly and that Nym and Bardolph "are sworn brothers in filching". (Later Bardolph and Nym are hanged for their misdeeds, and the boy, we assume, dies in the French raid cited in Act Four, Scene Seven.) Then the King threatens the people of Harfleur with a wholesale massacre: maidens will be raped, and babies and old people will be slain: the British troops will emulate "Herod's bloody-hunting slaughtermen" [III.iii]. (Matthew 2:16-18 tells us that King Herod ordered the slaughter of all the infants in Bethlehem in the hope of slaying Jesus.)

On the eve of Agincourt, Bates and Williams challenge the disguised monarch. Williams argues cogently that the King bears a heavy responsibility for the souls of the men who, serving him, die in battle unshriven: perhaps their souls go to hell – and then is it not the King's fault? (Williams speaks with firm clarity: here is a representative of the "common man" who is not caricatured or demeaned.) Henry argues that each man's soul is his own responsibility, but he is clearly shaken by the challenge, as is shown by his bitter soliloquy which begins thus:

> *Upon the King! Let us our lives, our souls,*
> *Our debts, our careful wives,*
> *Our children, and our sins, lay on the King!*
> *We must bear all. O hard condition...*
> *[IV.i]*

Here Henry reflects that he has inherited his father's guilt, for he has taken the throne that his father had seized from Richard. He continues:

> *Not today, O Lord,*
> *O, not today, think not upon the fault*
> *My father made in compassing the crown.*

Though he has demonstrated penitence and contrition,

> *all that I can do is nothing worth,*
> *Since that my penitence comes after all,*
> *Imploring pardon.*

Hal here believes that all his attempts to atone are worthless, since he retains the throne: true penitence would entail abdication.

During the battle itself, Henry's capacity for ruthlessness is both displayed and recalled. He twice gives the order that all the French prisoners are to be slain. Gary Taylor, in his Oxford edition of the play, adds, near the end of Act Four, Scene Six, the direction *"The soldiers kill their prisoners"*, claiming that this is why the opening of the scene specifies that prisoners are brought on; but Henry's injunction "Give the word through" (i.e. "Pass the order on") may suggest offstage killing.

Soon afterwards, Fluellen says that as Alexander killed his friend Cleitus, Henry has dealt similarly with Falstaff. Finally, the Epilogue calls in question the King's achievements: all the bloodshed, we are told, gained nothing in the long run.

How does Henry cope with his responsibililty?

One of the main themes of *Henry V* can be characterised as "passing the buck". Henry is always trying to resolve the obvious contradictions in his role: he is the son of a usurper who demands loyalty, and is a Christian monarch who is also a war-leader. He seeks to preserve his sanity and resolve inner divisions by making other people appear to take the responsibility or blame for his actions.

For example, he is anxious to involve the Archbishop of Canterbury in the decision to fight France. He warns the Archbishop that his justification for war must be honest, for "many now in health / Shall drop their blood in approbation / Of what your reverence shall incite us to" [I.ii]. The words "incite us" are important. Henry will make the decision, but he implies that a large part of the responsibility will be the Archbishop's.

Again, he will soon suggest that the Dauphin himself has made war inevitable. It is the Dauphin's insulting gift of tennis balls, Henry declares, that has provoked "wasteful vengeance" – and the Dauphin's "soul" will be "sore chargèd" for the vengeance: his mockery will cause slaughter in France [I.ii].

In dealing with Scroop, Cambridge and Grey,

Henry finds a cunning way of avoiding the blame. He tells them he is minded to be merciful to a man who recently "railed against" the King. Scroop, Cambridge and Grey say that, on the contrary, the King should punish him. Henry then arrests the three noblemen, saying that they are conspirators who will be sentenced to death for treason: and they themselves are responsible for the severe sentences: "The mercy that was quick in us but late, / By your own counsel is suppressed and killed" [II.ii]. This account, which Shakespeare found in the chronicles, uses an ancient plot-device. The *Motif-Index of Folk-Literature* lists it as type Q581, "Villain nemesis", in which a person

FALSTAFF AND SOCRATES

When describing the death of Falstaff, the hostess says: "I put my hand into the bed and felt [his feet], and they were as cold as any stone; then I felt to his knees, and so upward, and upward, and all was as cold as any stone." [II.iii.] Though potentially bawdy, this part of her account seems poignantly innocent; for, although "stone" could mean "testicle", that meaning does not fit here. Bizarrely, however, these odd details recall Plato's account of the death of Socrates.

Among grieving friends, the man who had given Socrates the poison "after a while... pressed his foot hard... and then his leg, and so upwards and upwards, and showed us that he was cold and stiff". Socrates had been sentenced to death for "irreligion and corrupting the young".

is condemned to a punishment he has suggested. The device is used in the old fable of "The Fox, the Wolf and the Lion". Henry, incidentally, terms Scroop's treachery "another fall of man", but in *Richard II* the Queen had with greater validity applied that image to Richard's downfall.

The three conspirators are rather implausibly penitent, and "rejoice" to be caught. The Chorus of *Henry V* suggests that they are motivated merely by love of French gold, but Cambridge in Act Two, Scene Two darkly hints at a different motive: that they were upholding the rightful claim of the Mortimers to the throne – and in Act Two of *Henry VI* it is made very clear that

---

If the linkage is not coincidental (and it seems too oddly specific to be coincidental), we are being invited to glimpse a likeness between these two apparently contrasting figures. Falstaff is deemed a corrupter of the young, too; but Hal is not corrupted by him. Socrates was not irreligious, but freely questioned a variety of beliefs. Falstaff seems irreligious in his conduct, but knows his Bible, and also freely questions a variety of beliefs. The linkage of the fat knight, who seeks pleasure and wealth, with the austere philosopher who values virtue above riches, is strange but telling; after all, each man has – in Socrates's image – served as "a gadfly" to the state: an enlivening irritant.

We are invited to imagine the ultimate Socratic dialogue: Socrates versus Falstaff: the topic "Pleasure or Virtue?". For once, it could not be a foregone conclusion that Socrates would win ∎

Cambridge is executed precisely for this reason. (Historically, it was the Mortimer who was Earl of March who himself betrayed the conspiracy to Henry.)

Henry's tactic of seeking to shift the blame for his actions on to others is evident throughout the play. Here are three other examples:

1. At Harfleur, Henry says that if the besieged people persist in keeping him out, then, when his troops do eventually burst in, there will be terrible slaughter: even old people and babies will

THE EFFEMINATE FRENCH

Alan Sinfield (in *Faultlines*) has cogently argued that, in *Henry V*, the superior masculinity of the English to the French is so insisted on as to appear the main validation of their claim to French territory. Near the end of *Richard II*, Henry IV had feared that his son was becoming an "effeminate boy". In *Henry V*, each side accuses the other of being effeminate; but the French generally "appear florid and effete": at Agincourt, for instance, the French have "gay new coats" while the English have "not a piece of feather", so the English appear the "real men". The French, realising this, express their apprehension in terms of lost power over women:

Our madams mock at us, and plainly say
Our mettle is bred out, and

be killed – and it will be the people's fault: "You yourselves are cause" [III.iii].

2. In the debate on the eve of Agincourt, Williams says the King is responsible if men die in battle without the last rites and are then damned. Henry argues that every man's soul is that man's responsibility. Henry, though apparently persuading Williams, is riled by the argument he makes, for Williams had tried to pass the buck to the King.

> they will give
> Their bodies to the lust of
> English youth,
> To new-store France with
> bastard warriors.
> [III.v]

When York and Suffolk are dying on the battlefield at Agincourt, York kisses Suffolk's lips, and thus "with blood he sealed / A testament of noble-ending love" [IV.vi]. Sinfield comments:

In such a context of devotion to the state, its fighting and its command structure, there is no damaging effeminacy in same-sex passion; it is women and popinjays that are the danger.

What, then, of the wooing and winning of Kate by Henry? Any son born of the marriage will have to be half-French to strengthen the claim to France, but since the play has repeatedly suggested that French manhood is tainted by effeminacy, retention of the conquered territory is put in jeopardy.

At the opening of *Henry VI Part 1*, the son of Katherine and Henry V is called "an effeminate prince"; and the French cities are lost through an "effeminate peace" ∎

3. After the great victory of Agincourt, Henry declares:

O God, thy arm was here;
And not to us, but to thy arm alone,
Ascribe we all.

[IV.viii]

It is not only a very pious response; it is a psychologically and morally salutary response: the credit for the victory – and the responsibility for the slaughter, including that of the prisoners – can be passed to God.

THE SIEGE OF HARFLEUR

At the siege of Harfleur, when Shakespeare's Henry threatens the citizens with indiscriminate massacres, he is faithfully echoing the threats made by the historic Henry.

The historic Henry claimed biblical warrant. He reminded them of Deuteronomy 20, which says that, after successful sieges of the cities of those people that the Lord God gives you as an inheritance, you shall save alive nothing that breathes. When the citizens of Harfleur persisted in resisting him, the historic Henry responded by "informing them of the penal edicts contained in the aforesaid law [of Deuteronomy] which it would be necessary to execute upon them as a rebellious people should they persist thus in their obstinacy". Ian Mortimer comments:

Why is Falstaff killed off?

The possible death of Falstaff is hinted at in the Epilogue to _Henry IV Part 2_:

> _"...if you be not much cloyed with fat meat, our humble author will continue the story, with Sir John in it... where (for anything I know) Falstaff shall die of a sweat, unless already [he] be killed with your hard opinions..."_

But while this suggests that Falstaff will die, his many fans would surely have been disappointed by the fact that the fat knight does not appear on

As Henry regarded the town as part of his inheritance from God this meant that the women and children, and even the cattle of the town, could also expect to be slaughtered along with the men.

Some citizens may have ruefully recalled that Jesus (Matthew 5: 44, 39) tells us to love our enemies and to turn the other cheek. (Jesus, however, did not love the money-changers but scourged them out of the temple: John 2: 14-16.) When Henry V likens his troops to "Herod's bloody-hunting slaughtermen", the paradox of Henry, the Christian martial leader, veers into self-contradiction: his men, he promises, will emulate the anti-Christian killers. In the Henry VI plays, we see that Hal's successor, Henry VI, is devoutly Christian and consistently pacific, but – and largely therefore – politically and martially incompetent ∎

stage in *Henry V*; his death-scene, though poignant, is reported. Dover Wilson has suggested that Falstaff had to be removed from the play because of the desertion or expulsion from Shakespeare's company of Will Kemp (or Kempe), who, Wilson believes, originally played the part. Michael Quinn shrewdly suggests an alternative explanation:

> ...the presence of the cynical and realistic old reprobate would have deflated disastrously the heroism of the warrior-king. Even his presence by report in the account of his death in Act II, is felt by some critics to convey a most telling criticism of the king, coming as it does immediately after Henry's own sermon to Scroop on the requirements of friendship.

Herschel Baker adds:

> Falstaff, with his tonic disrespect and his genius for subversion, would have been a greater threat to Henry V than all the French at Agincourt... Nym, Bardolph, and Pistol, deprived of their great chief, are only shabby clowns. Significantly, two of them are hanged, and the other slinks away...

The half-deranged ranting of Pistol, who is forced by Fluellen to eat a leek penitently, is no substitute for the shrewd reductionism of Falstaff, whose "Give me life" and denunciations of honour – including "I like not such grinning honour..." – would have provided incisively caustic opposition to Henry's patriotic oratory.

Falstaff is not available to humiliate Henry. But Henry does meet a possible moral vanquisher. The potential vanquisher is Williams, whose arguments have so unsettled Henry. Later, Henry and Fluellen try to buy his goodwill. Williams's last words in the play are: "I will none of your money" [IV.viii]. What happens after those words is a matter of interpretation. There are three options:

1. Williams nevertheless accepts Fluellen's shilling in addition to the gloveful of money promised by the King.
2. He keeps the gloveful but rejects Fluellen's shilling.
3. He rejects not only Fluellen's shilling but also the money promised by the King.

The last option, which some stage productions have enacted, preserves Williams's pride and enables him to transcend, morally, Henry's peculiarly contorted attempt to evade the showdown with him and to buy him off.

THE TRUTH ABOUT HENRY V

In Shakespeare's day, Henry V was popularly regarded as the glorious victor of Agincourt, the ideal monarch, perhaps even surpassing Edward III, whose troops, though greatly outnumbered, had defeated a French army at the Battle of Crécy (1346). Holinshed gives unstinting praise:

> This Henry was a king, of life without spot; a prince whom all men loved, and of none disdained; a captain against whom fortune never frowned, nor mischance once spurned; whose people him so severe a justice both loved and obeyed, and so humane withal, that he left no offence unpunished, nor friendship unrewarded... a pattern in princehood, a lode-star in honour, and mirror of magnificence.

The main story in *Henry V* maintains and magnifies this view of Henry, terming him "the mirror of all Christian kings" (here "mirror" means "ideal image") [II.Chorus].

Shakespeare depicts Henry as a uniter of the realm, for Scots, Irish and Welsh fight under his banner: this is shown by the presence of captains Jamy, Macmorris and Fluellen. In reality, in France, the French foes of Henry were reinforced by Scots. The Irish would long remain rebellious.

When the British capture Harfleur, Henry is seen to be merciful to the citizens; he says to his troops: "Use mercy to them all" [III.iii]. In fact, important citizens who failed to take an oath of allegiance to the British were sent to England for ransom, while the poorer citizens, women and children were "forcibly evacuated". While at Harfleur, the real Henry sent a personal challenge to the Dauphin to settle all the claims to France by single combat between the Dauphin and himself, in order to avert the shedding of much Christian blood. The Dauphin did not respond. Shakespeare omits this remarkably chivalric challenge.

In the play, the fictional Henry seeks to placate God by insisting that he has "interrèd new" Richard's body and has built chantries where priests sing for Richard's soul. The historic Henry indeed had Richard's body re-buried in state, and he arranged for a dirge and a requiem mass to be performed every week. The evident piety of Henry V, demonstrated in the play, was well attested by Holinshed and was historically factual. Bardolph is hanged for stealing a "pax" – an osculatory, a tablet to be kissed by the priest during the Mass. Holinshed says that one of Henry's soldiers was executed by strangulation for stealing a "pyx", a box in which sacred wafers are kept. The historic Henry had decreed that the looting of churches was punishable by death, and, on the march to Calais, a soldier found in possession of a stolen sacred vessel was hanged.

Near the end of the play, at the Treaty of Troyes, the betrothal of the French Princess, Katherine, to Henry appears to set the seal on an era of peace and harmony between Britain and France. On the death of the French King, the throne of France is to be occupied by Henry and his heirs. In reality, many Frenchmen did not accept the Treaty of Troyes; the fighting continued. The actual Treaty was signed in 1520, five years after Agincourt, whereas the play gives the impression that a much shorter time elapsed between the victory and the Treaty. Shakespeare as usual has compressed the time-scale, accelerating events.

The victory at Agincourt served to legitimate the rule of the real Henry V and his claims to France; and it lived on in British history and legend as a sign of divine approval of British courage. That's how it was rendered in poetry and ballads, notably in Samuel Drayton's "Ode to Agincourt" (c. 1605) and in the 17th-century ballad, "Agincourt, Agincourt! Know ye not Agincourt?"; and that's how it was taught in English schools in my childhood, in the 1940s.

What is the purpose of the Chorus?

"O for a Muse of fire, that would ascend / The brightest heaven of invention!": a stirring opening, which half-creates what it lacks: we see – as a heaven-storming fiery figure – the absence that the Chorus laments [Prologue].

The critic Catherine Belsey rashly claimed (in *Critical Practice*) that if a literary work draws attention to its own fictionality, that destroys its illusion. The Chorus of *Henry V* does the opposite: citing fictionality, it solicits our construction of the illusion; it draws attention to the *limitations* of theatrical representations of epic events, and begs the audience to make good these inadequacies by acts of imagination. "May we cram / Within this wooden O the very casques / That did afright the air at Agincourt?" ("Casques" are helmets.) The solution: "Piece out our imperfections with your thoughts."

The Chorus will return at the start of each subsequent act, to provide information about the passage of events and to repeat the appeal: "Still be kind, / And eke out our performance with your mind" [III]. Of course, the Chorus helps us to "eke out" the performance by evocative imagery: "Think, when we talk of horses, that you see them, / Printing their proud hoofs i'th'receiving earth" [Prologue]. The very word "printing" (alliterating so well with "proud") helps to generate distinctly the hoof-prints and thereby the imagined cavalry.

By frank admission of theatrical limitations, the Chorus wins our imaginative co-operation. It exhorts us to effort, and enthusiastically evokes the immense scale of the historic achievement. But something else is happening. This appeal to imaginative solidarity anticipates and strengthens Henry's climactic appeal to his "band of brothers". What the Chorus is doing to the imaginations of the audience, winning their co-operative assent, persuading them to make good the visual shortfalls, anticipates Henry's appeal to his hearers to make good, by their valour, the shortage in the British numbers. Complicity is established between audience and army.

There is a third effect, for thoughtful members of the audience. If imagination can give substance to the inadequate representations of royalty on stage, where we don't have real "princes to act / And monarchs to behold", perhaps in reality the mystique of monarchy and noble authority is dependent on persuasive performances and the credulity of the masses. James I would deem the monarch "one set on a stage". Henry V is a great performer, whether as judge, warlord or lover; but, as we suspend disbelief in the acted Henry V, we may increasingly be tempted to regard the real institution of monarchy as a tradition of play-acting which ultimately relies on public credulity.

HENRY V: WAR CRIMINAL?

In the play, Henry, on hearing that the French troops have been reinforced and are about to launch a new attack, gives the order that the French prisoners should be slain by their captors. He repeats that order on hearing that a French skirmish has seized the baggage and killed its boy-guardians. In reality, too, he gave the order twice. It seems that his soldiers were reluctant to forgo ransoms, so archers were deployed to do the killing. (Historians assume that prisoners of high rank would have been spared, because of their high ransom-value. The attack on the baggage probably occurred before Henry ordered the massacre). The literary critic John Sutherland points out that, in spite of Henry's command, at the end of the battle he is told that "prisoners of good sort" [IV. viii] number 1,500. Sutherland concludes:

> We may, then, assume one of two things. In the heat of battle Henry gives a command that may not have been carried out – at least not in full.

Alternatively, only the unregarded ordinary prisoners of war have been put to the sword. And who cares about them?'

A complicating factor is that when Henry is told by Exeter there are 1,500 prisoners "of good sort", Exeter adds "besides common men", implying an uncounted but possibly large number of surviving ordinary soldiers.

Modern historians say that the French prisoners probably numbered several thousand. Henry, learning that the French ahead were regrouping, possibly feared that the prisoners might rise and overwhelm their outnumbered and battle-weary captors, and he wanted all available troops to face the foe. Though ruthless, his death-command was, according to various commentators, justifiable in the circumstances: a pragmatic necessity. Margaret Labarge, for instance, says that the slaughter of the prisoners "was in conformity with the realities and conventions of medieval warfare", and Juliet Barker states that "in military terms... Henry's decision was entirely justified... Significantly, not one of [Henry's] contemporaries... criticised his decision." John Keegan speculates that the main aim was not to kill the prisoners but to frighten them into submission. He says that due to the sheer difficulty of killing so many in a short time, the numbers of slain prisoners may only have been hundreds.

Wavrin, however, an eyewitness, maintains that

the slaughter was thorough and "most pitiable"; Holinshed terms it "lamentable". Some modern commentators agree. At a mock trial of Henry V for war crimes in Washington in 2010, the court declared Henry guilty of the war crime of killing the prisoners – though the key criterion was variously reported as "the evolving standards of the maturing society" and "evolving standards of civilization". Ian Mortimer says: "By all the standards of the time, the killing was an ungodly act." It was "against the law of chivalry..., against Henry's own ordinances of war, and against Christian teaching". Yet, as Mortimer himself reminds us, the "ordinances" of war and Christian teaching could sanction the threatened slaying of all the citizens of Harfleur.

Shakespeare could have elided Henry's ruthless command at Agincourt, but chose not to. As presented in the play, it forms an important part of the critical subtext.

CONCLUSION

How sceptical was Shakespeare?

In Shakespeare's plays, the most explicit anti-religious views are usually, as we would expect, uttered by villains: for example, by Aaron, the wicked Moor of *Titus Andronicus,* by Richard III, or by Edmund in *King Lear*. When Macbeth says that life is "a tale / Told by an idiot, full of sound and fury, / Signifying nothing", this may be regarded as the sinful utterance – for it expresses despair – of an irredeemable sinner.

Something different, however, is happening with the speech by Henry IV – "O God, that one might read the book of Fate" (*Part 2,* III.i) – in which he reflects that time erodes continents, that "chance's mocks and changes" persist, and that "the happiest youth", on realising what is in store, would "sit him down and die". This is partly an utterance in character: the King is ageing and weary. It is deeply sceptical: there is no suggestion here of divine providence. It also, in its resonant emphasis on change and dissolution, anticipates the plangent scepticism of the wise Prospero, who, in *The Tempest*, after making the nuptial masque vanish, dares to declare:

> *The cloud-capped towers, the gorgeous*
> > *palaces,*
> *The solemn temples, the great globe itself,*
> *Yea, all which it inherit, shall dissolve,*
> *And, like this insubstantial pageant faded,*
> *Leave not a rack behind. We are such stuff*
> *As dreams are made on; and our little life*
> *Is rounded with a sleep.*

Prospero offers no suggestion whatever that providence oversees the process and that we awaken into eternal life. Like Henry IV, he offers a vision of vast-scale dissolution. Unlike Henry IV, his final emphasis is not on world-weary disillusionment, but simply on acceptance – part-stoical, part-melancholy – that after the dream of life we enter the sleep of death. Life is "rounded" with it: perhaps meaning "rounded off", aptly completed; more likely, "surrounded", encompassed.

The second tetralogy seems to dramatise endorsement of divine ordinance. We have noted that Richard's warnings of divine wrath to be

visited on the usurper are regarded as fulfilled, and Henry V's victory of Agincourt is repeatedly given the status of a virtual miracle. Nevertheless, the treatment of the supernatural in the second tetralogy is more circumspect and ambiguous – and less patriotic – than in the first, and from this we can infer a movement in Shakespeare's development towards ideological scepticism.

When we consider the tensions within *Henry V*, some conclusions emerge. Richard II was King *de*

King Henry V at the Battle of Agincourt, *1415, Sir John Gilbert (1817-97)*

jure, but erred in judgement, and failed as monarch. Henry IV, though an intelligent and circumspect ruler, was a usurper. Henry V, though charismatic and successful, had to act ruthlessly on numerous occasions. We may reflect: Henry V was a success – but who would ever wish to be him? If even the best of monarchs has to despatch so ruthlessly anyone seen as a threat, so much the worse for monarchy.

Another conclusion is this. As we see how the

justification for Henry's campaign in France is stage-managed, as we see the disparity between Henry's public assurance and private guilt, and as we see the legitimising effect of Henry's apparently pious accrediting of God with the great victory, then increasingly we may ask: "Where do morality and theology end, and where does ideology begin? Is it not possible that the moral and the religious may be subsumed under the category of ideology, that category consisting largely, though never entirely, of the doctrines which serve the powerful and which constantly seek the status of the natural, the obvious, the objective and the enduring?"

Such reflections are not anachronistic; they are no imposition of today's scepticism upon yesterday's notions. Protagoras (*c.* 490-420 B.C.) had declared "Man is the measure of all things", and "Concerning the gods, I have no means of knowing whether they exist". Thomas Hobbes (1588-1679) said: "Men measure, not only other men, but all other things, by themselves"; "*True and False* are attributes of Speech, not of Things"; "One man calleth *Wisdom*, what another calleth *fear*; and one *cruelty*, what another *justice*"; and "*Fear* of power invisible, feigned by the mind, or imagined from tales publicly allowed, [is] RELIGION; not allowed, SUPERSTITION". Falstaff's "What is honour? A word... Air" [*Part 1, V.i*] may seem cynically reductive, but it can be seen to usher Hamlet's "There is nothing either good or bad, but thinking makes it so" – a concise aphorism with vast implications.

In the 18th century, David Hume, in his *Treatise of Human Nature* (1739-40), will point out that one cannot deduce a conclusion containing a moral recommendation from premises containing statements of fact: there is always a logical void between "is" and "ought". People seek to bridge that void by means of rhetoric of one kind or another, perhaps religious or philosophical, perhaps by myths or manifestos: bridges of breath, Falstaff suggests.

What view of the world does Shakespeare leave us with in his second tetralogy?

When Shakespeare wrote his history plays, he was providing material for his company of players. He knew that they would use it diversely, in different locations, at different times. They would cut it, re-arrange it, and make additions and modifications. The political implications would change accordingly.

As the plays have proceeded through time, adaptations have multiplied, and so have the cultural forces which seek to voice themselves by means of the Shakespearian texts. Shakespeare operated within complicated conditions of censorship and within pressures to placate authority: *Macbeth* reveals a Shakespeare concerned to flatter James I; *Henry VIII* indicates a muzzled Shakespeare reluctant to make or provoke trouble. In the second tetralogy, he uses the "Tudor Myth" and the familiar image of Henry V, that glamorous warrior-king. But he also employs numerous questioning, critical features.

What results in these four plays is an enduringly complex and incisive analysis of power and power-seekers. Ian Mortimer, the historian, has said:

> Shakespeare was sufficiently inspired by Henry V to create a masterpiece: a sequence of four history plays that culminated in the triumph at Agincourt. Indeed, in that sense, the legend of Henry V really does live on, for Shakespeare's character has developed into a more important cultural figure in the modern world than the real Henry V. There are many biographies of Henry V, and there are many books on Agincourt; but there are even more on the Shakespeare play *Henry V*. Thus, as a leader of men engaged in a struggle against overwhelming odds, he has come to have meaning for the whole English-speaking world. And although it could be argued that the historical Henry does not deserve the credit for inspiring Shakespeare, it is fair to say that without that seed of greatness, the great work of literature would not have grown.

What makes it a "great work of literature" also includes, however, its estimation of the price paid in human terms for political success, and its ability to question definitions of the political.

The second tetralogy is *fully* political because it appears to *exceed* the political. Shakespeare knew what he was doing when he planted in the heart of this vast panorama of power his most subversive comic character, Falstaff. Rightly, we remember the heroic oratory of Hal; but Shakespeare obliges us to recall the dying Falstaff, who childishly babbled of green fields. The gardener in *Richard II*, Davy in *Henry IV Part 2*, the argumentative Williams and the doomed boy in *Henry V*: such apparently minor characters are an essential part of Shakespeare's rich and profound dramatisation of politics and power. Against the stirring oratory of the "band of brothers" speech, he sets the boy's "I would give all my fame for a pot of ale, and safety" [III.ii]. Against Henry V's "Cry 'God for Harry, England, and Saint George!'" [III.i] echoes Falstaff's "Give me life" [*Part 1*, V.iii].

As Shakespeare developed the second tetralogy, he increasingly relished both the politicising of aesthetics and the aestheticising of politics. He politicised the aesthetic by showing that even the comical escapades of Falstaff have their political implications. He aestheticised the political by invoking perspectives which question the nature and the extent of the political. The Chorus of *Henry V* shows that Shakespeare could deliberately and explicitly put political discourse between the sceptical and aestheticising quotation-marks of the avowedly fictional. The audience is exhorted to confer seeming reality, by acts of imagination, upon the fiction – fiction which shows how people may regard fiction as truth. He thereby implied the subjection of the whole area of ideological discourse (political, ethical, religious) – its ultimate subjection to the human imagination.

Shakespeare, like Iago, was attracted by Janus, the two-faced god who presides over paradox; but, as a practical man of the theatre, he knew that the full truth lay in the power of Proteus – not the treacherous character in *The Two Gentlemen of Verona*, but the god who eludes capture by constantly changing shape. The truth, in other words, is implicit in the protean diversity of the Shakespearian scripts and their trammelled or untrammelled re-enactments. William Blake says: "All deities reside in the human breast"; Shakespeare implies: "All ideologies reside in the human imagination."

CENSORSHIP IN
SHAKESPEARE'S TIMES

In Sonnet 66, Shakespeare complains that some
things are so bad that they make him wish he were
dead. Among them are the following:

> *strength by limping sway disablèd,*
> *And art made tongue-tied by authority,*
> *And folly, doctor-like, controlling skill...*

All three lines can be regarded as a bitter comment
on censorship, including censorship of the theatre.
But they are paradoxical. And you have probably
already sensed why. Because we can read them.
These lines have not been censored. In Stalin's
Russia, a complaint about censorship would itself
be censored; not so in Elizabethan or Jacobean
England. Matters could, therefore, have been worse.
Nevertheless, the climate of censorship has
complicated Shakespeare's treatment of history.

Have you ever read an Elizabethan play called
Liberty Unchained? That's a play in which a merry

Puritan, a heroic Catholic, a generous Jew and a virtuous atheist combine forces: they assassinate Queen Elizabeth and declare Britain a democratic republic. Rejoicing crowds praise them and dance in the streets. No, I haven't read it either. It's a play which the censorship of the day would never have permitted, so nobody would have dared to write it. On the other hand, we can read a play about the assassination, long ago, of Julius Caesar, or another about the overthrow of Richard II.

In Shakespeare's day, censorship was wielded by all levels of society, from the top to the bottom, from the monarch to the apprentices. Apprentices could boo, jeer and be disruptive if they did not like a play. At a higher level, the business of censorship was characterised by muddle, inconsistency, severity and laxity: a mixture of Kafka and *Alice in Wonderland*. Cyndia Clegg has estimated that, between 1585 and 1625, only 30 per cent of books had official authorisation. Sanctions, however, were numerous. If a play gave political offence, the playwright or playwrights could be jailed. If a company of players gave offence, they could be jailed or put out of business: they could lose their patronage, and their theatre could be ordered to close.

The grounds of offence were numerous. Attacks on the monarchy asked for trouble. So did satiric treatment of Scots after 1603, during the time when a Scottish monarch, James VI, surrounded by Scottish courtiers, occupied the British throne as James I. In 1605, for contributing to the play *Eastward Ho*, Ben

Jonson and George Chapman were jailed. That play was deemed a satire on James and his courtiers. Portrayals of rebellions and insurrections were also perilous. In the 1590s, when Sir Edmund Tilney was Master of the Revels, one of the plays he read was *Sir Thomas More* (attributed to Anthony Munday and others). Tilney wrote in the play's margin: "Leave out the insurrection wholly and the cause thereof." Yet in the surviving material, the insurrection scene – probably by Shakespeare – is not left out wholly: it was simply rewritten, and the new version was inserted over the old.

Generally, in Shakespeare's plays, characters who overthrow a legitimate ruler tend either to perish themselves as a result, as do Macbeth, Brutus and Cassius, or at least to suffer at length, as does the constantly-worried Henry IV. Would-be revolutionaries may be satirised, as in *Henry VI Part 2*.

Nevertheless, the plays of Shakespeare's day do not give the general impression of a theatre in a straitjacket. Janet Clare reports that in 1606 George Calvert, who was later to be a secretary of state, wrote thus to a friend about plays in London's theatres:

> The players do not forbear to represent upon their stage the whole course of the present time, not sparing either king, state, or religion, in so great absurdity, and with such liberty, that anyone would be afraid to hear them.

In ways varying from the direct to the oblique,

numerous plays offer radical questioning of authority (whether religious or political) and of the ways of justice. *King Lear* not only voices challenges to judicial authority; it also exposes the fallibility of a monarchical system, and even questions, with bitter irony, any belief in a benevolent God or gods. *Troilus and Cressida* voices the traditional platitudes about hierarchical order and the need to respect it; but those platitudes are put into an utterly ironic context, so that today this play seems peculiarly contemporary in its scepticism. The wiles and hypocrisies of politicians are exposed in numerous plays: notably in *Richard III*, *Julius Caesar*, *Troilus and Cressida*, and throughout the second tetralogy.

Of course, a playwright could respond to political censorship by producing works which comment obliquely rather than directly on current affairs, and Shakespeare's plays give clear instances of people who are skilled in eliciting messages which cannot be openly expressed (Aaron, Brutus and Claudius, for instance). As Polonius says: "By indirections find directions out."

In civilised societies, freedom of speech is never absolute; it is always freedom of speech within the confines of the law. The censor may not always have tied Shakespeare's tongue. He may frequently have helped Shakespeare to speak with many tongues, some of them forked.

1377 Richard II crowned

1399 (Sept) Richard II deposed

1399 (Oct) Henry IV crowned

1402 Hotspur defeats Scottish army

1403 (21 July) Battle of Shrewsbury

1405 Rebellion by Archbishop of York, Mowbray and others.
(York and Mowbray executed in June.)

1413 Henry IV dies, Henry V crowned

1415 (Aug-Sept) Siege of Harfleur

1415 (Oct 25) Battle of Agincourt

1422 Henry V dies, succeeded by Henry VI

1558 Elizabeth I becomes Queen

1577 Holinshed's *Chronicles* published. The second edition (1587)
was an important source for Shakespeare's second tetralogy

circa 1591 Shakespeare writes *Henry VI Part 1* (probably with
Thomas Nashe and others).

c. 1592 *Richard III*

c. 1595 *Richard II*

c. 1597 *Henry IV Part 1*

c. 1598 *Henry IV Part 2*

1599 *Henry V*

Baker, Herschel, commentaries in *The Riverside Shakespeare,* Boston: Houghton Mifflin, 1974.

Bakhtin, Mikhail, *Rabelais and His World* [1965], London: MIT Press, 1968.

Barber, C. L., *Shakespeare's Festive Comedy* [1959], Cleveland and New York: Meridian, 1966.

Barker, Juliet, *Agincourt*, London: Abacus, 2006.

Berry, Ralph, *On Directing Shakespeare,* Harmondsworth: Penguin and Hamish Hamilton, 1989.

Carlyle, Thomas, *On Heroes, Hero-Worship and the Heroic in History* [1841], London: Chapman and Hall, 1904.

Clare, Janet, *"Art made tongue-tied by authority": Elizabethan and Jacobean Dramatic Censorship,* Manchester U. P., 1990.

Clegg, Cyndia Susan, "Liberty, License and Authority" in *A Companion to Shakespeare*, ed. David Scott Kastan, Oxford: Blackwell, 1999.

Coyle, Martin, ed., *William Shakespeare: "Richard II",* Cambridge: Icon Books, 1998.

Dawson, Anthony B., and Yachnin, Paul, ed., Shakespeare: *Richard II,* Oxford U. P., 2011.

Dickson, Andrew, *The Rough Guide to Shakespeare,* London: Rough Guides, 2005.

Digges, Leonard: quoted in the *Introduction to Shakespeare: Henry IV Part One*, ed. David Bevington, Oxford U. P., 1998.

Dollimore, Jonathan, and Sinfield, Alan, ed., *Political*

Shakespeare: New Essays in Cultural Materialism, Manchester U.P., 1985.

Dutton, Richard, and Howard, Jean E., *A Companion to Shakespeare's Works: Vol. 2: The Histories*, Oxford: Wiley-Blackwell, 2003.

Greenblatt, Stephen, "Invisible Bullets" in *Political Shakespeare*, ed. J. Dollimore and A. Sinfield, Manchester U. P., 1985.

Hazlitt, William, *The Selected Writings of William Hazlitt, Vol. 1*, ed. Duncan Wu, London: Pickering and Chatto, 1998.

Healy, Margaret, *William Shakespeare: "Richard II"*, Plymouth: Northcote House, 1998

Hunter, G. K., ed., *Shakespeare: Henry IV, Parts 1 and 2: A Casebook*, London: Macmillan, 1970.

Johnson, Samuel, *Johnson on Shakespeare,* ed.Walter Raleigh, Oxford U. P., 1908.

Keegan, John, *The Face of Battle: A Study of Agincourt, Waterloo and the Somme* [1976], Harmondsworth: Penguin, 1978.

Knowles, Ronald, *Shakespeare and Carnival: After Bakhtin*, Basingstoke: Macmillan, 1998.

Labarge, Margaret W. *Henry V*, London: Secker & Warburg, 1975.

Law, R. A., "Structural Unity in the Two Parts of *Henry IV*": *Studies in Philology*, Vol. 24 (1927), pp. 223-242.

Lee, Sir Sidney, Introduction to *King Henry V*, ed. Lee, New York: Sproul, 1908.

Margolies, David, "Henry V and Ideology" in *Shakespeare on Screen: The Henriad*, ed. S. Hatchuel and N. Vienne-Guerrin, Rouen: Laboratoire Eriac, 2008.

McAlindon, Tom, *Shakespeare's Tudor History: A Study of "Henry IV Parts 1 and 2"*, Aldershot: Ashgate, 2001.

Montagu, Elizabeth, quoted in the Introduction to Shakespeare: *Henry IV Part One*, ed. David Bevington, Oxford U. P., 1998.

Morris, Corbyn, quoted in *William Shakespeare: The Critical Heritage, Vol. 3*, ed. Brian Vickers, London: Routledge, 1975.

Mortimer, Ian, *1415: Henry V's Year of Glory,* London: Vintage, 2010.

Myers, A. R, *England in the Late Middle Ages,* Harmondsworth: Penguin, 1956.

Norbrook, David, "A Liberal Tongue: Language and Rebellion in Richard II" in *Shakespeare's Universe: Renaissance Ideas and Conventions*, ed. John M. Mucciolo, Menston: Scolar Press, 1996.

Palmer, Sir Thomas, quoted in the Introduction to Shakespeare: *Henry IV Part One*, ed. David Bevington, Oxford U. P., 1998.

Patterson, Annabel, *Censorship and Interpretation*, Wisconsin U. P., 1984.

Quinn, Michael, ed., *Shakespeare: "Henry V": A Casebook*, London: Macmillan, 1969.

Saul, Nigel, *Richard II* [1997], New Haven and London: Yale U.P, 1999.

Schanzer, Ernest, *The Problem Plays of Shakespeare* [1963], London: Routledge & Kegan Paul, 1965.

Sinfield, Alan, *Faultlines*, Oxford U.P, 1992.

Sprague, A. C., *Shakespeare's Histories: Plays for the Stage*, London: Society for Theatre Research, 1964.

Sutherland, John, and Watts, Cedric, *Henry V, War Criminal? and Other Shakespeare Puzzles*, Oxford U. P, 2000.

Taylor, Gary, Introduction to *Henry V*, ed. Taylor, Oxford U.P, 1994.

Tillyard, E. M. W, *Shakespeare's History Plays* [1944], Harmondsworth: Penguin, 1964.

Traversi, Derek, *Shakespeare from "Richard II" to "Henry V"*, London: Hollis & Carter, 1958.

Vickers, Brian, ed., *Shakespeare, The Critical Heritage*, 6 vols., London: Routledge & Kegan Paul, 1974-81.

Wilson, J.D, *The Fortunes of Falstaff* [1943], Cambridge U.P, 1979.

All quotations from *Richard II*, *Henry IV* and *Henry V* are taken from the Wordsworth texts edited by Cedric Watts.

INDEX

First published in 2014 by
Connell Guides
Artist House
35 Little Russell Street
London WC1A 2HH

10 9 8 7 6 5 4 3 2 1

A CIP catalogue record for this book is available from the British Library.
ISBN 978-1-907776-29-8

Design © Nathan Burton
Assistant Editors:
Katie Sanderson, Paul Woodward & Pierre Smith Khanna
With assistance from Lydia Symonds

Printed in Italy by LEGO

www.connellguides.com